THE GO...

FLORENCE

Brief illustrated guide to the city.
The churches, museums and monuments.

© Copyright by Casa Editrice Bonechi - Firenze - Italia
E-mail:bonechi@bonechi.it Internet:www.bonechi.it Internet:www.bonechi.com

Publication created and designed by Casa Editrice Bonechi
Graphic design: Sauro Giampaia. Make-up: Federica Balloni
Texts by Various authors. Editing: Anna Baldini, Federica Balloni
Cover: Manuela Ranfagni. Drawings: Stefano Benini

Printed in Italy by Centro Stampa Editoriale Bonechi - Sesto Fiorentino

Photographs from the Archives of Casa Editrice Bonechi taken by
Gaetano Barone, Marco Bonechi, Carlo Cantini, Serena de Leonardis, Andrea Fantauzzo, Foto Scala, Paolo Giambone, Francesco Giannoni, Dario Grimoldi, Italfotogieffe, M.S.A., Andrea Pistolesi, Antonio Quattrone
Page 27 above, courtesy of Cassa di Risparmio di Firenze

The publisher apologies for any omissions and is willing to make amends with the formal recognition of the author of any photograph subsequently identified.

ISBN 88-476-1509-7

HISTORICAL SURVEY

Florence lies at the foot of the Tusco-Emilian Appennines, in the large plain cut by the Arno river and surrounded by hills. After being inhabited in prehistoric times, during the 8th century BC, an Italic people, with a Villanovan culture, settled in the area between the Arno and the Mugnone rivers, but little is known of these remote times.

In 59 BC, the Roman city was founded, with the square ground plan of the castrum. The decumanus was laid out along what are now the Via del Corso, the Via degli Speziali and the Via Strozzi, while the ancient cardus corresponds to the line between Piazza San Giovanni, the Via Roma and the Via Calimala. Marcus Aurelius (or Diocletian) chose it as the seat of the Corrector Italiae, the governor responsible for Tuscany and Umbria. With the arrival of the Barbarians, Florence was first besieged by the Ostrogoths of Radagaisus (405), who plundered the surrounding countryside, although Florence managed to resist protected by Stilicho's troops intlicting an overwhelming defeat on the enemy. Next came the Byzantines, who occupied Florence in 539, and the Goths who took over the city in 541. Under Lombard domination (570), the city managed to safeguard its autonomy, while under the Franks, the number of inhabitants diminished, and the city lost most of its territory. Around the year 1000, the ascent of Florence began and continued through various centuries in spite of numerous controversies, wars and internal struggles. New walls were built around the city, new civic and religious buildings went up, and at the same time the arts, literature, and trade continued to prosper. In 1183, the city became a free Commune, although it had already actually availed itself of this freedom for many years. The first clashes between two factions, the Guelphs and the Ghibellines, date to those years. The first were followers of the Pope, the second of the Emperor. These clashes were to lacerate the civil fabric of the city up to 1268. The Ghi-

bellines were the first to gain advantage and expelled the Guelph families from the city in 1249. But Florence's roots were Guelph, and the followings years these won. The Ghibellines sought refuge in Siena, where they were overtaken by the Guelph troops, who were, however, badly

beaten in the battle of Montaperti. As a result, Florence was once more Ghibelline for various years until the battle of Benevento (1226), when the Guelphs once more defeated their bitter rivals, once and for all. Despite the unstable social and political situation, this period witnessed an upsurge in the arts and in literature. This was the time of Dante and the "Dolce Stil Novo", of Giotto and Arnolfo di Cambio. In the 15th century, the city's rise continued. Florence was a trading city, but also the new

here during this period, when Florence was at its highest prestige. In 1737, to the Medici succeeded the house of Lorraine, and the government continued along the lines of a moderate liberalism, although by that point the great period of Florentine culture was fading away. In 1860, during the Risorgimento, Tuscany was annexed to the kingdom of Italy with a plebiscite. For a brief period, Florence became the capital of the new nation. During World War II, serious damage was inflicted on the historical centre and various important buildings were lost. Despite this and the flood, which invaded the city in 1966, Florence has retained its charm.

cradle for Italian and eventually European culture. Many powerful families (Pitti, Frescobaldi, Strozzi, Albizi) contended the supremacy of the city. Finally, a powerful family of bankers – the Medici – distinguished themselves. The first to govern would have been the founder Cosimo I, later known as the Elder. His successors were to govern up to the first half of the 18th century, making Florence the leading city during the period of Humanism and the Renaissance. Great personalities, such as Leonardo da Vinci and Michelangelo, worked

BAPTISTERY OF ST. GIOVANNI

The Florentine Baptistery seems to have been built originally around the 4th-5th century, in an area occupied by a large Roman *domus*, and the peripheral parts extended as far as the area later occupied by Santa Reparata. The site was near the northern gate of Roman Florence (located between the Baptistery and the *Via Cerretani*), and the religious building was always octagonal in plan, with a semi-circular apse and set on a podium with steps. In the 11th century, the Baptistery became the city cathedral, since Santa Reparata was being rebuilt. San Giovanni (the Baptistery) too was refaced both inside and out, while in 1128, the smooth pyramidal roof was finished and topped by a lantern with columns (1150).

The **apse** – also called *Scarsella* – was rebuilt in a square shape in 1292, and in 1293, when the work

carried out by the corporation of the *Arte di Calimala* (wool merchants' guild) was finished, the Baptistery looked as it does today. The building, where the Florentine Republic invested its knights, is still today faced on the **exterior** by green and white marble. Each side is divided into three areas by pilaster strips supporting an entablature below and round arches with windows above. The higher entablature has an attic divided into blind compartments.

The three bronze **doors** are particularly important. The *South door,* which is the oldest and is decorated with scenes from the *Life of St. John the Baptist* and the *Allegories of the Theologian and Cardinal*

Andrea Pisano, South door *(1330-36).*

Virtues, is by Andrea Pisano (1330-1336). The *North door,* with *Stories from the New Testament, Evangelists and Doctors of the Church* is by Lorenzo Ghiberti (1403-1424), with the help of Donatello, Bernardo Ciuffagni, Paolo Uccello and Bernardo Cennini. And lastly, the *Eastern door,* known as the *Gates of Paradise* with

Gate of Paradise:

The Creation of Adam and Eve, Original Sin, The Fall from the Earthly Paradise.

The Battle with the Philistines, The Slaying of Goliath.

Lorenzo GHIBERTI
• Gate of Paradise • (1425-52)

The door on the east side of the Baptistery was described by Michelangelo as the Gate of Paradise, not only because of its beauty but also because of the symbolic importance of its position. The iconographical cycle represented in the decoration of the door wings is spread over 10 panels with bas-reliefs representing Stories from the Old Testament enclosed within a frame of 24 niches made up of full-length statuettes reproducing Biblical figures alternating with 24 medallions containing small heads of Artists, including a self-portrait of Ghiberti himself. The original panels, made in embossed gilded bronze, are on display in the Museo dell'Opera del Duomo following a meticulous restoration.

GATE OF PARADISE

The Creation of Adam and Eve, Original Sin, The Fall from the Earthly Paradise.

The Sacrifice of Noah and his Family after Leaving the Ark, The Drunkenness of Noah.

The Birth of Esau and Jacob, Selling of the Birthright, Isaac and Esau Ordered to Go Hunting, Esau Hunting, Rebecca Advises Jacob, The Deceit of Isaac.

Moses Receives the Ten Commandments on Mount Sinai.

The Battle with the Philistines, The Slaying of Goliath.

The Work of the First Men, The Sacrifice of Cain and Abel, The Murder of Abel, The Lord Punishes Cain.

The Angels Appear to Abraham, The Sacrifice of Isaac.

Joseph Sold to the Merchants, The Discovery of the Golden Cup in Benjamin's Sack, Joseph Reveals Himself to his Brothers.

The People of Israel in Jordan, The Fall of Jericho.

Solomon and the Queen of Sheba

The mosaics of the cupola of the Baptistry.

The tomb of the anti-pope John XXIII.

ten panels (now replaced by copies) representing *Stories from the Old Testament* is by Lorenzo Ghiberti, and is considered one of the greatest masterpieces of 15th-century sculpture.

The **interior** has an inlaid pavement with decorative motives of eastern style. On the walls from left to right you may admire a Roman *sarcophagus,* the *sarcophagus of Bishop Ranieri* and the *tomb of the antipope John XXIII* (1427), designed by Michelozzo and Donatello, who also executed the lying statue. The Baptistery also houses a marble baptismal font dating 1371, attributed to the school of Pisa. The tribune in the apse has Byzantine style mosaics on the vault, dating 1225 by Fra' Jacopo.

Other mosaics cover the entire **cupola**, at which Florentine artists, probably helped by Venetian craftsmen, worked between the 13th and the 14th century. These artists include Cimabue, Coppo di Marcovaldo and Gaddo Gaddi. The tondo above the apse represents *Christ* surrounded by scenes of the *Last Judgement.* The opposite side contains *Stories of the Baptist,* scenes from the *Life of Christ,* and from the *Life of Joseph,* as well as *Stories from Genesis.* The *Angelic Hierarchies* are represented around the lantern.

The interior of the Baptistry.

CATHEDRAL

The Cathedral of Florence, dedicated to *Santa Maria del Fiore*, is the fruit of the commitment of a large number of artists who worked on it over a period of centuries. At the end of the 13th century, Florence, then a Commune, was already flourishing and the build-up area had spread considerably. The extant cathedral of Santa Reparata was by then too small to house the citizens, and no longer sufficiently prestigious for the city. In his *Cronache,* Giovanni Villani writes that "the citizens came to an agreement on the renewal of the principal church of Florence, which was of a simple form and small in comparison to a city of this kind; and they gave orders to make it larger and set the façade further back, and to make it all in marble and with sculptured figures". In 1294, the Art Guilds, that supported the government, decided that Arnolfo di Cambio should construct a new cathedral, and when the building was completed, the preexisting church should be torn down. At the time **Santa Reparata** was situated where the front part of the cathedral now stands. The Church had been built in the 4th-5th centuries on the ruins of a Roman *domus,* and

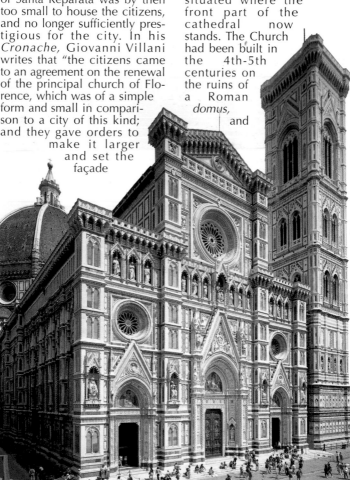

it had a nave and two aisles with a single apse. During the Byzantine wars, the church was destroyed, and then rebuilt between the 8th and 9th centuries. Although the perimeter was basically the same, two side chapels were added to the structure and the columns were replaced by pilasters with strips. Between the years 1000 and 1100, a crypt with a raised choir was created in the area of the apse, which was flanked by two bell towers outside. The new cathedral building yard grew around and inside this church and although work continued for decades, Santa Reparata continued being the cathedral until 1375.

Work on the new cathedral, begun on September 8, 1296, was interrupted in 1302 when Arnolfo di Cambio died. His place as masterbuilder was taken by Giotto, in 1334. However, the social situation and various natural calamities (the economic crisis due to the bankrupt of the Bardi and Peruzzi banks, the flood of 1333, the popular uprisings and the plague of 1348) slowed down the construction. After Giotto's death in, 1337, Andrea Pisano, Francesco Talenti and Giovanni di Lapo Ghini worked on the Duomo. In 1375, Santa Reparata was demolished to the height of two and a half metres and the plans for the cathedral were changed, so that part of Arnolfo's structure was torn down.

The building was finally finished with the exception of the **dome**, which had been included in the original project but turned out to be more difficult to build than planned. The competition for the dome was won in 1420 by Brunelleschi, who proposed to build the enormous aerial structure without the use of fixed centring, thanks to the adoption of interconnected ribbing and herringbone bricks. The dome was finished in 1434, and the cathedral was consecrated in 1436, 140 years after it had been begun.

The **lantern** at the top of the dome was also designed by Brunelleschi, but as Vasari

Tombstones in the Crypt of Santa Reparata.

Giotto's campanile: in the sixteen niches of the lower band statues of the *Prophets,* the *Sibyls* and *John the Baptist* were placed. Among those of the various Prophets, Donatello sculpted the statue of *Habakkuk,* the original of which is in the Museo dell'Opera del Duomo together with the original panels and other statues.

Brunelleschi's eight-sided **dome**.

In the left aisle, two interesting **frescoes** portraying equestrian monuments, one dedicated to John Hawkwood, the work of Paolo Uccello, the other to Niccolò da Tolentino, by Andrea del Castagno, as well as a painting representing *Dante and the Divine Comedy* by Domenico di Michelino.

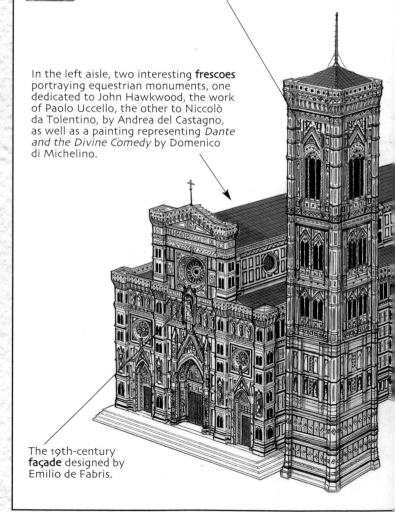

The 19th-century **façade** designed by Emilio de Fabris.

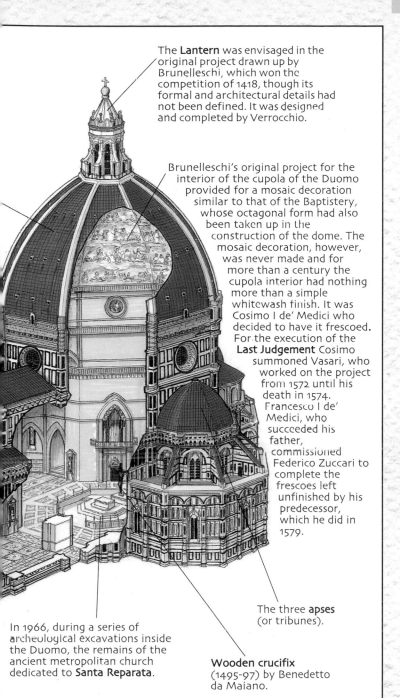

The **Lantern** was envisaged in the original project drawn up by Brunelleschi, which won the competition of 1418, though its formal and architectural details had not been defined. It was designed and completed by Verrocchio.

Brunelleschi's original project for the interior of the cupola of the Duomo provided for a mosaic decoration similar to that of the Baptistery, whose octagonal form had also been taken up in the construction of the dome. The mosaic decoration, however, was never made and for more than a century the cupola interior had nothing more than a simple whitewash finish. It was Cosimo I de' Medici who decided to have it frescoed. For the execution of the **Last Judgement** Cosimo summoned Vasari, who worked on the project from 1572 until his death in 1574. Francesco I de' Medici, who succeded his father, commissioned Federico Zuccari to complete the frescoes left unfinished by his predecessor, which he did in 1579.

The three **apses** (or tribunes).

In 1966, during a series of archeological excavations inside the Duomo, the remains of the ancient metropolitan church dedicated to **Santa Reparata**.

Wooden crucifix (1495-97) by Benedetto da Maiano.

notes, "because he was now old and would not live to see the lantern finished he stipulated in his will that it should be built with the model and the written instructions that he left; otherwise, he insisted, the fabric would collapse as it was vaulted in an ogive and needed the weight pressing down on top in order to strengthen it. He failed to see this edifice completed before he died, but he raised it to a height of several feet...".

Arnolfo's **façade** was torn down in 1587, and designs for a new one abounded. Not until 1871 were the plans by De Fabris approved, and they were then carried out in 1887. This façade, which is the one we now see, employed the same types of marble as those used in the revestment of the sides: Carrara white, Prato green and Maremma rose. Above the three portals, with *Stories from the Life of the Virgin*, there are three lunettes with, left to right, *Charity,* the *Madonna with the Patrons of the City,* and *Faith.* The gable of the main entrance has a *Madonna in Glory.* Statues of the *Apostles* and of the *Virgin* are on the frieze running between the side rose windows and the central one. The tympanum, with a bas-relief of *God the Father*, is set above a row of busts of artists. Four doors open in the sides of the

A view of the facade and dome of the cathedral.

The interior of the cathedral.

cathedral articulated by pilasters and tall mullioned windows with two lights. On the bell tower side, there are the *Bell tower Door* and the *Canons Door*, while on the other side are the *Balla Door* and the *Mandorla Door*. The latter is 15th-century, and is decorated in the lunette with a mosaic of the *Annunciation* by Ghirlandaio, a tympanum by Nanni di Banco, and *statues of the Prophets* by the young Donatello.

The **interior** is very spacious, both in height and width, following the dictates of Italian Gothic architecture. The three broad aisles are divided by composite pillars from which spring large moderately pointed arches. The spaciousness of the bays unifies the area of the cathedral, enhacing its width. At the bottom of the naves there is a large area occupied

by the high altar, around which there are the three apses, each divided in five parts. Under the stained glass windows designed by Ghiberti, and the clock with Paolo Uccello's *Prophets* (1443), the **interior façade** bears the 14th-century lunette with the *Coronation of the Virgin* by Gaddo Gaddi, and the *tomb of Antonio d'Orso,* by Tino di Camaino, 1321 circa. The **left aisle**, apparently very simple, contains various masterpieces: at the beginning is the aedicule with a statue of *Joshua,* by Ciuffagni, Donatello and Nanni di Bartolo, and the neighbouring *Aedicule of St. Zanobius* painted at the end of the 14th century by Vanni del Biondo. Between Benedetto da Maiano's *bust of A. Squarcialupi* and Ciuffagni's *Aedicule with David* (1434) there are the two *equestrian monuments,* once frescoed, of

Giovanni Acuto (John Hawkwood) and *Niccolò da Tolentino*. The former was painted by Paolo Uccello in 1436, representing the soldier of fortune in such a severe pose that it communicates immobility, while in the latter (1456), Andrea del Castagno has a livelier plasticity giving a sense of vitality to the knight. In front of the arch of the fouth bay, under the stained-glass window designed by Agnolo Gaddi, are the panels with *St. Cosmas and St. Damian* (by Bicci di Lorenzo, 15th century), and *Dante Alighieri* (by Domenico di Michelino, 1465).

In the left tribune, is Lorenzo di Credi's *St. Joseph* in the first room on the left, and once it contained Michelangelo's marble *Pietà*, now in the nearby Cathedral Museum. Two marble aedicules flank the door of the **New Sacristy** surmounted by a lunette in glazed terra-cotta by Luca della Robbia. This *Resurrection*, which Luca made in 1444, is exalted by an ascending movement that is both linear and sculptural, and is enriched by colour. On the opposite side, beyond the high altar – a 16th-century work by Baccio Bandinelli – there is the door to the **Old Sacristy** with Luca della Robbia's other lunette of the *Ascension*. The right tribune contains a Giottesque fresco with the *Madonna* and a *St. Philip* by Bandini. Beyond this, in the south aisle, is a painting of *St. Bartholomew Enthroned* by Franchi (15th cent.) and the aedicule with a *Prophet* by

The interior of the cathedral dome.

Dante and the Divine Comedy *by Domenico di Michelino.*

Equestrian monument to Niccolò da Tolentino *by Andrea del Castagno (1456).*

Paolo Uccello, Equestrian monument to John Hawkwood *(1436).*

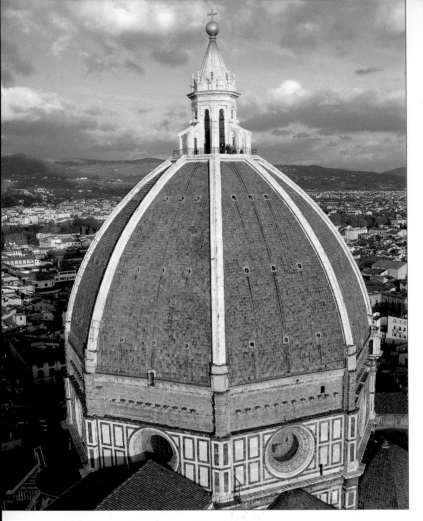

Brunelleschi's eight-sided dome.

Nanni di Banco (1408), set between the medallions with *Giotto* (by Benedetto da Maiano, 1490) and with *Brunelleschi* (by Buggiano, 1446). Here, a modern staircase descends to the pre-existant church of Santa Reparata. The great **dome**, which Brunelleschi had conceived as bare, was however painted by Giorgio Vasari and Zuccari between 1572 and 1579. Scenes from the *Last Judgement* are set in three concentric bands with the *Prophets* at the top of the vault in a trompe l'oeil lantern with a railing. A passageway set in the dome, leads to the frescoes – recently restored – and, from the terrace above the high altar, continues up to the lantern at the top of the cathedral.

GIOTTO'S CAMPANILE

The cathedral bell tower was begun in 1334 by Giotto, masterbuilder for the construction of the Cathedral. Until his death, in 1337, he built the bottom part of the bell tower composed of two closed stories decorated with hexagonal and rhomboid reliefs, by Andrea Pisano, Luca della Robbia, Alberto Arnoldi and workshop. The relief panels on the lower band, now replaced by casts, represent the *Life of Man in the Creation and in the Human Arts* executed by Andrea Pisano and Luca della Robbia on Giotto's designs. The theme was influenced by the fact that Giotto had been named master builder by the Corporation of the Arts, which at the time controlled the government in Florence. It was therefore to compliment his patrons that he included the following subjects in this order: *Tilling of the Land, Sheepraising, Music, Medicine, Hunting, Weaving, Legislation, Mechanics, Navigation, Justice, Agriculture* and *Theater.* The upper row, which dates from the second half of the 14th century, represents the *Planets,* the *Virtues,* the *Liberal Arts* and the *Sacraments.*

The two upper stages were finished by Andrea Pisano, who took Giotto's place. He created a series of sixteen niches between the pilaster strips which contained *statues of the Prophets, Sibylls* and the *Baptist,* surmounted by an equal number of false niches. Between 1350 and 1359, Francesco Talenti finished the bell tower, adding two levels with the two gabled mullioned windows with two lights with their lovely twisted columns and the story with the single mullioned window with three lights. On the top, more than 81 metres high, he created the large terrace supported by small arches and with an openwork balustrade.

The statue of Habakkuk by Donatello, one of the 16 statues once located in the niches of Giotto's campanile and now housed in the Museo dell'Opera del Duomo.

CATHEDRAL MUSEUM
(MUSEO DELL'OPERA DEL DUOMO)

The Cathedral Museum is installed behind the apse of the cathedral. The entrance is surmounted by a fine *Bust of Cosimo I* by Giovanni Bandini. **Inside** there are numerous examples of Romanesque sculpture, statues and architectural pieces from the ancient façade of the Duomo and the Baptistery. Among the finest statues on the

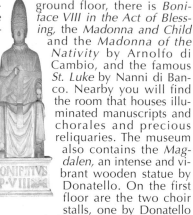

The statue of Boniface VIII *by Arnolfo di Cambio.*

Donatello, Mary Magdalen *(1453-55).*

ground floor, there is *Boniface VIII in the Act of Blessing,* the *Madonna and Child* and the *Madonna of the Nativity* by Arnolfo di Cambio, and the famous *St. Luke* by Nanni di Banco. Nearby you will find the room that houses illuminated manuscripts and chorales and precious reliquaries. The museum also contains the *Magdalen,* an intense and vibrant wooden statue by Donatello. On the first floor are the two choir stalls, one by Donatello and the other by Luca della Robbia, and various statues once set on Giotto's campanile. They are of the prophets *Habakkuk, Jeremiah* and another *Prophet,* all by Donatello, *Abraham* and *Isaac* by Nanni di Bartolo. In the room to the right is the fine *Altarpiece of St. John the Baptist,* a large monument on which Michelozzo, Verrocchio, Antonio del Pollaiolo and Bernardo Cennini collaborated. On either side are the statues of *Our Lady of the Annunciation* and the *Archangel Gabriel* by Jacopo della Quercia. In the room to the left are the original relief panels from Giotto's bell tower, made for the two tiers: they are by Andrea Pisano, Alberto Arnoldi and Luca della Robbia. Other examples of painting and sculpture include a noteworthy diptych with scenes from the *Lives of Christ and the Madonna,* it is of Byzantine school and dates from the late 13th century; Michelangelo's *Deposition,* formerly in the Cathedral (the central figure is supposed to be a self-portrait), and the Baptistery altar, in silver, with gilding and enamel.

Luca Della Robbia's choir loft.

The choir loft by Donatello.

MICHELANGELO
Pietà (1550-53)

This marble sculpture, which Michelangelo never completed, was, in the artist's intentions, supposed to have adorned his own funerary chapel in Santa Maria Maggiore in Rome. In actual fact it never left Florence, and only in the 18th century was it set up in one of the chapels of the left tribune of the cathedral, from where it was removed in more recent times to its present position in the Museo dell'Opera del Duomo. In the centre of the group is the figure of the dead Christ supported by Nicodemus, in whom it is traditionally believed the sculptor portrayed his own likeness, by the Madonna and by Mary Magdalen, finished by one of Michelangelo's pupils. The figure of Christ, whose arm (later restored) and left leg were destroyed by the artist in a fit of rage, is, with its modelling, the fulcrum of the composition. The unfinished state of the sculpture confers to the whole a heightened sense of dramatic force.

PIAZZA DELLA SIGNORIA

It is among the most beautiful Italian squares, and it occupies a large area. The piazza was enlarged later, between the 13th and 14th centuries, thanks to the demolition of the houses of various Florentine Ghibelline families, including the Uberti and the Foraboschi. The imposing complex of **Palazzo Vecchio** towers over the piazza on the north side. To the right of the façade of Palazzo Vecchio is the lovely **Loggia dei Lanzi**, a late Gothic structure by Benci di Cione and Simone Talenti (1376-91). To the left of the palace, is the beautiful *Fountain of Neptune*, or *Fontana di Piazza*, by Bartolomeo Ammannati (1563-75) and, to one side, the *Equestrian Statue of Cosimo I* (1594) by Giambologna.

FONTANA DEL BIANCONE (THE NEPTUNE FOUNTAIN)

This very scenic sculptural group was carried out between 1563 and 1575; the powerful figure of *Neptune* standing out in the centre of the Fountain, is not one of Ammannati's best works (the artist may have been inspired by a drawing of Leonardo). Best are the bronze statues representing *River Allegories* of satyrs and nymphs by Ammannati and some of his young collaborators, including Giambologna.

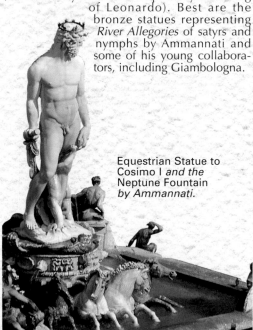

Equestrian Statue to Cosimo I *and the* Neptune Fountain *by Ammannati.*

Victory (1533-34) by Michelangelo, sculpted for the tomb of Pope Julius II

Elevated Tribune "dell'Udienza"

Vasari's **frescoes** of the conquest of the Tuscan provinces by the Medici

Equestrian statue of Cosimo I by Giambologna

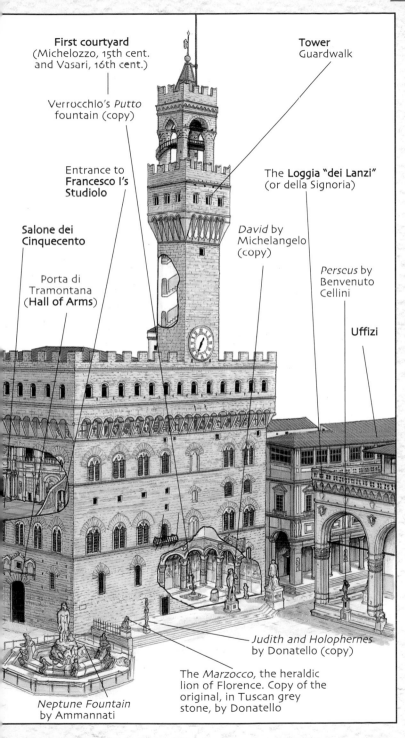

First courtyard
(Michelozzo, 15th cent. and Vasari, 16th cent.)

Verrocchio's *Putto* fountain (copy)

Entrance to **Francesco I's Studiolo**

Salone dei Cinquecento

Porta di Tramontana (**Hall of Arms**)

Tower
Guardwalk

The **Loggia "dei Lanzi"** (or della Signoria)

David by Michelangelo (copy)

Perseus by Benvenuto Cellini

Uffizi

Judith and Holophernes by Donatello (copy)

The *Marzocco*, the heraldic lion of Florence. Copy of the original, in Tuscan grey stone, by Donatello

Neptune Fountain by Ammannati

25

EQUESTRIAN STATUE OF COSIMO I DE' MEDICI

The monument is on the left of Palazzo Vecchio. It has a very dignified and noble air in the proud pose of the *condottiere* and in the powerful muscles of the horse, which Giambologna, as a mature artist, was capable of creating (1594). The bas-reliefs of the pedestal show the *Entry of Cosimo into Siena, Pio V Giving Cosimo the Insignia of the Grand Duke, The Tuscan Senate Giving Cosimo the Title of Grand Duke.*

LOGGIA DEI LANZI

Built by Benci di Cione and Simone Talenti between 1376 and 1391, it consists of large round arches on compound pillars, although there is also emphasis on horizontal rhythms. Of late Gothic style, the Loggia is very elegant. The fine reliefs above the pillars are allegories of the *Virtues,* designs by Agnolo Gaddi. On either side of the stairs two *lions* flank the access: one is an example of classic art, the other is by Flaminio Vacca (1600).

Various outstanding examples of sculpture are preserved **inside** the Loggia: in the foreground, on the right, the *Rape of the Sabine Women* by Giambologna (1583), a plaster copy of which is in the Galleria dell'Accademia; in the centre are **Hercules and the Cen-**

The Loggia dei Lanzi and Rape of the Sabines *by Giambologna (1583).*

*tau*r, also by Giambologna (1599), *Ajax bearing the body of Patroclus*, a Greek group with later additions, and the *Rape of Polyxena* by Pio Fedi (1866). In the foreground, on the left, is **Perseus**, Cellini's most famous work.

Perseus *by Benvenuto Cellini (1545-54).*

Palazzo Vecchio: bottom, Verrocchio's Putto with a Dolphin, a copy of which decorates the fountain in the courtyard designed by Michelozzo and Tower by Arnolfo di Cambio.

PALAZZO VECCHIO

Begun in 1294, as a palace-fortress for the residence of the Priors, Arnolfo di Cambio conceived the building as a large block crowned by merlons.

The characteristic feature is the powerful thrust of the **Tower** rising up above the palace and similar in style to the upper part of the mansion. The building is in rusticated ashlars of "pietra forte" giving the large three-storied building with its fine mullioned windows with two lights within round arches an air of severity.

A row of statues is set in front of the building. On the left, at the foot of the palace is the *Marzocco,* the lion, the heraldic symbol of the city (a copy of Donatello's original of 1438, now in the Museum of the Bargello); to the right of the Marzocco is the copy of Donatello's *Judith* (1460), followed by a copy of Michelangelo's *David* and *Hercules and Cacus* (1534) by Baccio Bandinelli. On the left of the observer is the large *Fountain of Neptune.*

Immediately **inside** is the first **courtyard** rebuilt by Michelozzo. The columns were stuccoed and gilded and the walls were frescoed with *Views of the Austrian Cities* by Vasari on the occasion of the wedding of Francesco de' Medici with Joan of Austria, in 1565. At the centre there is a *Fountain* by Francesco del Tadda with a *Winged putto holding a spouting fish* (1467) by Andrea del Verrocchio. Under the portico there is a fine sculpture of *Samson and the Philistine* by Pierino da Vinci.

After the courtyard, two spacious flights of stairs (by Vasari) lead on each side to the large **Salone dei Cinquecento** built by Cronaca and decorated by a team of painters chosen by Vasari. The ceiling is decorated with allegorical panels of the *Triumph of the Grand Duke Cosimo I*; the four *Quarters of the City* (in the medallions in the ceiling); the sixteen *Cities of the Duchy* (in the compartments at the four corners), the six *Stories of Medici Tuscany* (in the rectangular and square compartments of the central part), the seven *Stories of the Wars for the Conquest of Pisa* (in the rectangular, octagonal and square compartments on the left side), and the seven *Stories of the Wars against Siena* (in the panels on the right side).

On the entrance walls are the large allegories of *Cosimo I*

A view of Piazza della Signoria with 'David' standing at the entrance to Palazzo Vecchio.

The Salone dei Cinquecento.

Hercules and Diomedes *by Vincenzo De Rossi.*

founding the Order of the Knights of St. Stephen, by Passignano, and further down, the three great *Stories of the Conquest of Pisa.* These are followed by three marble sculptures: the *Three Labours of Hercules* by Vincenzo De Rossi, and the *Statue of Cosimo I* by Baccio Bandinelli. The back wall has *Leo X* by Baccio Bandinelli in the central niche; in the side niches are *Giovanni delle Bande Nere* and *Alessandro de' Medici* by Bandinelli, a niche on the right contains *Charles V Crowned* (Bandinelli and Caccini). On the wall facing the entrance, above left, *Cosimo receiving the Insignia of the Grand Duchy from Pope Pius V,* by Cigoli; above right, *Cosimo acclaimed Duke of*

The Studiolo of Francesco I.

Florence, also by Cigoli; further down, three large *Stories of the Conquest of Siena* by Vasari. Michelangelo's sculpture of *Victory* is on the wall to the right.

A door at the far right of the entrance leads to the **Studiolo of Francesco I**, a small chamber created by Vasari. The walls are lined with panels painted by Bronzino, Naldini, Santi di Tito, Stradano and with bronze statues by Giambologna, Ammannati, Vincenzo De Rossi. The small study is also decorated with stuccoes, and frescoed in the lunettes with the portraits of the *Grand Duke Cosimo* and *Eleonora of Toledo,* by Bronzino. A small staircase leads to another chamber known as **Tesoretto of Cosimo I** (by Vasari) with the Grand Duke's magnificent desk.

From the Hall of the Fivehundred, a decorated corridor leads to the **Salone dei Due-**

cento (1441) by Giuliano and Benedetto da Maiano, with a fine carved coffered ceiling by Michelozzo; on the walls there are tapestries woven in the Medici tapestry workshops on designs by Bronzino.

Entrance to **Leo X Apartments** is from the Hall of the Fivehundred. These include many rooms rich in paintings and frescoes: the *Hall of Leo X*, frescoed in 1560 with scenes from the *Life of the Pope*; the *Hall of Clement VII*, the *Hall of Giovanni delle Bande Nere*, the *Hall of Cosimo the Elder*, the *Hall of Lorenzo the Magnificent*, the *Hall of Cosimo I*. A staircase to the second floor leads to the **Elements Apartments**, by Battista del Tasso. The name derives from the *Allegories of Earth, Air, Water and Fire* painted in the first

room, by Vasari. Mention should also be made of other charming rooms: the *Room of Hercules*, the *Terrace of Saturn*, the *Terrace of Calliope*.

A gallery overlooking the Hall of the Fivehundred, leads to the **Apartment of Eleonora of Toledo** by Vasari, which begins with a beautiful *Chapel* frescoed by Bronzino. Then comes the *Room of the Sabines* (once reserved to the ladies of the court), the *Room of Esther* (dining room), the *Room of Penelope*, the *Room of Gualdrada* (the bedroom of the Grand Duchess). A *Chapel* known as the *Cappellina della Signoria*, frescoed by Ridolfo del Ghirlandaio (1514) and with a tender *Holy Family* by Mariano da Pescia on the altar, leads to the *Audience Hall*, with its fine carved ceiling by Giuliano da

The 'Cappella dei Priori' (Prior's Chapel).

Sala di Clemente VII. Vasari's reconstruction of the Siege of Florence *by the Imperial troops of Charles V in 1529-30 offers a minutely detailed record of 16th-century Florence.*

Sala dei Gigli, Judith and Holofernes *by Donatello (1455-60).*

Maiano (1478). The *Hall of the Gigli,* so-called because of its decoration of golden fleur de lis on a blue field, leads to the *Sacristy,* with the *Portrait of Niccolò Machiavelli,* by Santi di Tito. The bronze original of Donatello's *Judith,* restored and presented to the public in 1988, is on exhibition in the Hall of the Gigli. In the adjacent *Cloak-room,* embellished with 53 painted panels in the doors of the wardrobes, is the large *Map of the World* by Danti. A staircase leads to the **Quarter of the Mezzanino** (Apartments), and to the old *Gallery* from where one can go to the **Tower** of the palace, where Cosimo the Elder and Savonarola were imprisoned, and from which it is now possible to see a magnificent view of the city.

THE UFFIZI

The Palazzo degli Uffizi was commissioned to Giorgio Vasari by Cosimo I de' Medici in 1560, and completed, according to the original project, by Alfonso Parigi and Bernardo Buontalenti in 1580. It was built next to Palazzo Vecchio, following the latter's enlargement, to house the offices of the city magistracies. The palace of the Uffizi is a long, U-shaped structure, almost a theatrical enclosure, which extends as far as the north bank of the Arno. Building it involved sacrificing the glorious old church of **San Piero Scheraggio**, which was partly demolished and partly incorporated into the new edifice. On the ground floor Vasari built lofty arcades supported by alternating Doric columns and pilasters and above them a loggia, which initially had no specific use. It was Cosimo's successor, Francesco I de' Medici, who decided that the loggia should have the present-day function of a Gallery, and he commissioned Buontalenti to build the **Tribune**, where the Grand-duke ammassed numerous precious objects and ancient medals. Francesco also set out the first corridor of the gallery, placing in it the Medici family's collection of Greek and Roman statues, from which the *Galleria delle Statue* gets its name. After Francesco's death, Ferdinando I de' Medici had

The loggia of the Uffizi in a detail of The Goldsmith's Workshop *by Alessandro Fei (ca. 1570).*

the classical statues of Villa Medici transferred from Rome to Florence, thus further enriching the collection, to which were soon added also the finest pieces from the Medici Armoury and a collection of Mathematical Instruments.

The Gallery benefited from other substantial acquisitions in the 17th century, notably that of the wife of Ferdinando II de' Medici, Vittoria della Rovere, whose dowry contained the immense patrimony of her grandfather Federico, Duke of Urbino, including precious works by Raphael and Titian. The other important acquisition enriching the Medici collections was Cardinal Leopold's bequest to his nephew Cosimo III de' Medici, who built new rooms in order to accommodate it, and constructed a new and more monumental entrance to the Uffizi. Cosimo's daughter Anna Maria Ludovica, last of the Medici and widow of the Elector Palatine, added works by German and Flemish masters, and through a family Pact of 1737 settled that the art collections belonging to her family be left to the city of Florence. The **Galleria degli Uffizi** thus became the city's first art museum, a museum that in the following decades continued to grow and inspired the creation of other prestigious Florentine museums.

A portion of the Uffizi overlooking the Arno.

THE GALLERY

The Museum of the Uffizi Gallery has known a period of unbroken development since the 16th century, one marked by successive acquisitions of works and collections. This has involved the progressive enlargement of the space required to house them. Thus, the area of the museum, which in the past occupied only that part named 'The Gallery', was extended to incorporate also part of the Vasari Corridor and the Tribune. In 1988 the rooms of the ground floor and the first floor (originally used as offices of the Signoria) became available following the transferral of the State Archives, at the Uffizi since 1852, to a new site.

As part of the **"Nuovi Uffizi"** project, the subsequent triplication of space enables the numerous works kept in the storerooms of the museum to be displayed. In the rooms the paintings and sculptures are arranged chronologically and are displayed in clearly defined sections which correspond to the centuries of their respective production. Thus it is possible to admire, in succession, the sections dedicated to the **Painting of the 13th and 14th century**, the **Painting of the 15th century**, **North European Painting**, the **Tribune**, **Painting of the 16th century** and **Painting of the 17th and 18th century**.

PAINTING OF THE 13th AND 14th CENTURY

The history of Italian and particularly Tuscan art in the 13th and 14th centuries is the history of an evolution from forms ideologically and technically independent of the Byzantine tradition to the more humanly concrete and spatially defined forms of Western art. Mosaic and fresco painting were still the most commonly used techniques during this period, although painting on wood, in which colours were applied in tempera, was more and more widely adopted. Generally speaking, however, modes of pictorial expression evolved imperceptibly and even within mosaic and fresco cycles dramatic and popularesque elements introducing a more concrete sense of reality became in-

DUCCIO DI BUONINSEGNA, **Rucellai Madonna** (1285)

GIOTTO, **Ognissanti Madonna** (ca. 1303)

creasingly common. In the same way painting on wood continued in its conquest of human values, portraying actions and sentiments that could be fully understood, particularly with the help of a progressively defined sense of space. The same subjects, given their almost exclusively ecclesiastical destination, appeared again and again: Crucifixes in which Christ was presented as *triumphans*, but also and increasingly often as *patiens*, Enthroned Madonnas, and large figures of Saints surrounded by small

Ambrogio LORENZETTI
Presentation in the Temple
(1342)

Pietro LORENZETTI
Madonna and Child Enthroned with Angels (14th C.)

Taddeo GADDI
Madonna and Child Enthroned with Angels and Saints (1355)

37

GENTILE DA FABRIANO
Adoration of the Magi (1423)

MASACCIO and MASOLINO
Madonna and Child with Saint Anne and Five Angels (1424-25)

scenes depicting episodes from their lives. Among the most important artists who distinguished themselves in the field of the arts during these two centuries were Cimabue, Giotto and his followers.

PAINTING OF THE 15th CENTURY

Three main factors characterized the 15th century in Florence: first, the city's experi-

PIERO DELLA FRANCESCA
Portraits of the Duke and Duchess of Urbino (ca. 1465-70)

Filippo LIPPI
Madonna and Child with Angels (ca. 1445)

ence of late Gothic culture; second, the cultural revival that intensified with the rise of Humanism and with the later Renaissance; and third, the spread of the Renaissance itself. The leading figures representing the International Gothic style in Florence were Lorenzo Ghiberti in sculpture, particularly the period of his first door for the Baptistery, and Lorenzo Monaco in painting. The influence of these artists was responsible for the creation of a Florentine late Gothic school that lasted throughout the first half of the 15th century. But in early 15th-century society other social forces sought new forms of expression and this led to profound changes that in Florence were introduced by Filippo Brunelleschi, Donatello and later Masaccio. In the midst of the numerous vicissitudes that made the Florentine environment of those years unique and distinguished the leading artists of the time,

BOTTICELLI, **Primavera** (1482-83)

BOTTICELLI, **The Birth of Venus** (1484-86)

PAOLO UCCELLO, **Battle of San Romano** (1456)

one painter emerged, Filippo Lippi, who succeeded in inventing a style that proved enormously successful and who propagated those artistic ideals which later became the common heritage of Florentine Renaissance society and which after 1460 witnessed the flourishing of important figures like Antonio del Pollaiolo, Verrocchio, Botticelli and Leonardo. This great period ended with the death of Lorenzo il Magnifico and the rise of Savonarola.

LEONARDO, **Annunciation** (1472-75)

NORTH EUROPEAN PAINTING

The first relations and exchanges between Germany and central and northern Italy date from the last decade of the 15th century. The protagonist of the first journey to Italy was Albrecht Dürer of Nuremberg, who later became the founder of the German Renaissance. The five paintings by Dürer at the Uffizi are important examples of this painter's art. The Uffizi has other paintings of considerable quality by Lukas Cranach the Elder, and has recently increased its already large group of German painters with the acquisition of two masterpieces by the leading exponent of the Danubian school, Albrecht Altdorfer. Also from the area of Germany is Hans Holbein the Younger, whose long residence in Basle gives him an intermediate position between the Rhine region, France and Italy. As regards Flanders and Holland, on the one hand the two regions were closely linked, on the other two clearly distinct artistic orientations were forming, this being due mainly to the tendency of Dutch painters to break away from their Flemish origins. After this, North European artists, especially those active in the wealthiest and most important city of the Low Countries, Antwerp, aspired to assimilate various

ALBRECHT DÜRER, **Adoration of the Magi** (1504)

ROSSO FIORENTINO, **Musician Angel** (before 1530)

fundamental principles established by Italian art and humanism such as the supremacy of the human figure. Towards the middle of the century Italian painting triumphed throughout the rest of Europe.

BRONZINO
Portrait of Eleonora of Toledo with her Son Giovanni (1545)

THE TRIBUNE

The Tribune (Room 18) was built for Grand-duke Francesco I de' Medici by Bernardo Buontalenti and completed in 1589. It was furnished in such a way as to accommodate both sculptures and paintings of large and small dimensions. It was also intended as an anthology of the treasures of the Medici collections and a reflection of late 16th-century culture and artistic tastes at the end of the Renaissance. Over the centuries the treasures of the Tribune have been displayed in various ways. The present arrangement is a compromise between some aspects of the original layout and a selection of paintings, a somewhat debatable initiative since some of them have never before been displayed here. However, the choice is not entirely arbitrary since it does reflect the Trubune's original function. Indeed, the Tribune today presents a panorama of mature 16th-century art as it developed in Tuscany and Rome.

PAINTING OF THE 16th CENTURY

Giorgio Vasari was certainly right when he celebrated the 16th century as the one in which the figurative arts in Italy reached perfection. Italian art in fact achieved complete mastery both of style and human form. Beauty and intelligence were fused in what seemed an unrepeatable union. 16th-century art did not develop uniformly. On the contrary, few centuries have witnessed such a rapid succession of changes

MICHELANGELO
Tondo Doni
(ca. 1506)

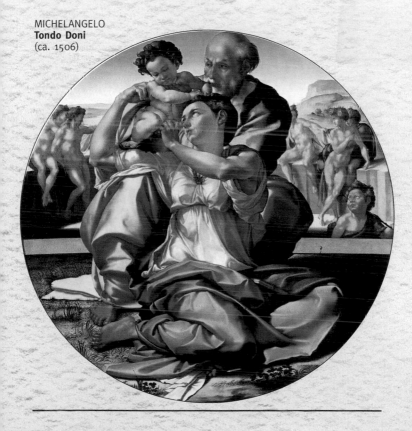

RAPHAEL, **Madonna of the Goldfinch** (1506)

or the simultaneous existence of widely differing tendencies. Private and public space began to expand for political, economic and above all religious reasons, which had an enormous bearing on developments in the artistic world. In Florence, Rosso Fiorentino and Pontormo were the main exponents of the crisis of Classicism and of the tormented artistic vicissitudes in Italy in the first half of the 16th century.

Mannerism was destined to become a national phenomenon with its centre of activity in Rome, where its greatest representative was certainly Michelangelo. After the middle of the century a new force, the Church of the

ANDREA DEL SARTO
Madonna of the Harpies
(1517)

Counter-Reformation, made its appearance with different historico-artistic objectives and the prevalence of ideals of abstract simplicity, even austerity. Vasari was one of the protagonists of this period in Florentine art. The end of the century witnessed the crisis of Mannerism, with two partly parallel developments: a return to the ordered, harmonious, reassuring world of early Florentine classicism, and the discovery of Venetian painting with its irresistible naturalistic charge.

TITIAN, **Venus of Urbino** (1538)

CARAVAGGIO
Bacchus
(late 16th C.)

PAINTING OF THE 17th AND 18th CENTURY

The rooms in the Uffizi dedicated to the 17th and 18th centuries are an illustrious record of the participation of the last Medici rulers in the period of expansion of European collectionism which had started at the end of the 16th century. Although Cosimo III de' Medici was more interested in Dutch masters, it was he who acquired two valuable paintings by Rubens in 1686. The Uffizi also entered into possession of some important works by Van Dyck and by those artists who represented the poles of the revival that took place in Italy at the end of the 16th century: Caravaggio and Annibale Carracci. The interest of the Medici family in North European painting is amply reflected in the Florentine collections and concerns particularly various members of the grand-ducal family. In the first half of the 17th century this interest - which significantly regarded Cardinal Carlo and Cosimo II de' Medici, both sons of a north European woman, Christine of Lorraine - was to a large extent focused on landscapes. Another aspect of Medicean collectionism in keeping with the taste of the European princely courts of the late 17th century is represented by the series of small-format Dutch paintings and with interior scenes, bought by Cosimo III during his journeys to Holland, or coming from the Elector Palatine and his wife Anna Maria Ludovica. The room dedicated to the 18th century is a limited representation of what the Uffizi possesses of this century, a century which saw the end of the Medici dynasty and the reforming presence of the Lorraine family. Artistic activity was deeply affected by these events and was manifested in the falling off of the patronage of the last Medici and the emigration of numerous artists.

CHURCH OF SANTA CROCE

The church is one of city's largest and has a neo-Gothic **façade** added in the 19th century heavily decorated.

The building, attributed to Arnolfo di Cambio (13th cent.), has a majestic **interior** with a nave separated from the two aisles by slender octagonal pilasters supporting the broad pointed arches with a double cornice. At the end of the nave, with its open timber roof, is the transept with the chapels. The internal wall of the façade contains a stained-glass window with the *Deposition,* done from a cartoon by Lorenzo Ghiberti. Below, on the right is the *monument to Gino Capponi* by Antonio Bortone (1876), while on the left, is the *monument to G.B. Niccolini,* historian and poet, by Pio Fedi. On the first altar, in the **right aisle**, is a *Crucifixion* by Santi di Tito (1579),

while the famous *Madonna del Latte,* a bas-relief by Antonio Rossellino, is on the first pillar. On the wall are the *funeral monuments to Michelangelo Buonarroti,* by Vasari (1564), *to Dante Alighieri,* by Stefano Ricci (1829); *to Vittorio Alfieri,* poet and patriot, by Canova (1803), and *to Niccolò Machiavelli* by Innocenzo Spinazzi (1787). The octagonal *Pulpit* by Benedetto da Maiano (1475), a sculptural ensemble with *Scenes from the Life of St. Francis,* is at the third pillar. Behind the fifth altar there are remains of frescoes by Andrea Orcagna, while further on, you can admire a tabernacle in *pietra serena* with the *Annunciation* by Donatello (1472-76), a very animated monument; the *tomb* of the historian *Leonardo Bruni,* by Rossellino; the *funeral monument to Gioacchino Rossini*

Church of Santa Croce: the Cappella Maggiore.

and the one to the poet *Ugo Foscolo* by Antonio Berti (1939).

In the **Castellani Chapel**, or *Chapel of the Sacrament*, in the right arm of the transept, is the cycle of frescoes with scenes from the *Lives of SS. Nicholas of Bari, Anthony Abbot, John the Evangelist and John the Baptist*, by Agnolo Gaddi (1385); a fine *Crucifix* by Niccolò Gerini is at the altar, while on the walls are terra-cotta *Saints* from the Della Robbia workshop. Further on, at the head of the transept, is the **Baroncelli Chapel**. Outside is the magnificent *tomb*, in Gothic style, of the Baroncelli family, and a lunette with a *Madonna* by Taddeo Gaddi. Inside, on the right wall, the fine fresco of the *Madonna of the Girdle with St. Thomas,* by Bastiano Mainardi (1490), and the cycle of *Scenes from the Life of Mary,* by Taddeo Gaddi, on the other three walls; on the altar is the fine *Coronation of the Virgin* by Giotto.

Michelozzo's portal, in the right side of the transept, leads to the **Sacristy**, originally built in the 14th century, with *Scenes from the Passion* by Niccolò Gerini on the right wall. From the back wall of the Sacristy you enter the **Rinuccini Chapel**, with scenes from the *Lives of the Virgin and St. Mary Magdalen* by Giovanni da Milano, and a fine altarpiece by Giovanni del Biondo (1379). The Sacristy also leads to the **Medici Chapel** or *Novices' Chapel,* built by Michelozzo for Cosimo the Elder. Here you can admire various works by Della Robbia, including some *busts*, an altarpiece, and a shrine by Verrocchio; to the right is the *monument to Francesco Lombardi*

The interior of the basilica of Santa Croce.

Giorgio Vasari, Sepulchral monument to Michelangelo *(1570).*

Giulio Foggini, Funerary monument to Galileo Galilei *(1574-1642).*

Church of Santa Croce: the Cappella Baroncelli.

Anonymous artist, St. Francis and twenty stories of his life *(13th C.), Bardi Chapel.*

with a magnificent bas-relief that may be by Donatello.

Various chapels with important works of art open off the back of the central part of the transept: the **Velluti Chapel**, with *Scenes from the Legend of St. Michael*

Archangel, perhaps by Cimabue; the **Calderini Chapel**, later **Riccardi**, with a lunette-shaped vault with *Scenes from the Life of St. Andrew Apostle* by Giovanni da San Giovanni; the **Giugni Chapel**, later **Bonaparte** with the *monument to Carlotta Bonaparte,* by Lorenzo Bartolini; the **Peruzzi Chapel**, with the magnificent *Scenes from the Life of St. John Evangelist* by Giotto (1320); the **Bardi Chapel**, with the *Scenes from the life of St. Francis* by Giotto (1318) and, above the external arch, the *Miracle of the Stigmata,* while the *Allegory of Chastity, Poverty* and *Obedience,* and the *Triumph of the Saint* were frescoed on the vaulting by Giotto. On the altar is a panel of *St. Francis and twenty stories of his life* of Luccan school, late 13th century; then comes the **Cappella Maggiore** with the *Legend of the Cross* (1380) by Agnolo Gaddi. On the altar is a polyptych with the *Madonna* and *Saints* by Niccolò Gerini, and above the altar a *Crucifix* of the school of Giotto; next comes the **Tosinghi Chapel**, with a polyptych by Giovanni del Biondo on the altar; the **Capponi Chapel**, with the *monument to the Virgin Mary and her Dead Son* by Libero Andreotti (1926); the **Ricasoli Chapel**, with two 19th-century canvases of *Scenes from the Life of St. Anthony of Padua;* the **Pulci Chapel**, with a glazed terra-cotta altarpiece by Giovanni della Robbia and noteworthy frescoes on the walls (the *Martyrdom of SS Lawrence* and *Stephen* by Bernardo Daddi); the **Bardi di Vernio Chapel**, frescoed with scenes from the *Life of Pope Sylvester* (by Maso di Banco) and with two niche-

Giotto, Stories of St Francis of Assisi *(after 1317), Bardi Chapel.*

shaped 14th-century *tombs* on the left wall.

At the far end of the left arm of the crossing are the **Niccolini Chapel**, with statues by Pietro Francavilla, paintings by Alessandro Allori (1588) on the altars, and a fine cupola frescoed by Volterrano (1660); the **Bardi Chapel** (the last to the left of the crossing), with Donatello's magnificent *Crucifix* (1425), and the **Salviati Chapel**, with the *Martyrdom of St. Lawrence* by Jacopo Ligozzi (1600) on the altar.

The *tomb-stones* of the humanist *Carlo Marsuppini* by Desiderio da Settignano, and *Galileo Galilei* (1642) by Foggini are in the **left aisle**. Access to the **First Cloister** is outside through the *Door of the Martello* to the right of the façade. The 14th-century cloister is articulated by fine arcades. At the back of the cloister, is the marvelous **De' Pazzi Chapel**, which Filippo Brunelleschi designed on a central plan with a dome and a lantern. Outside, a Corinthian porch is set in front of the façade, with a frieze containing roundels with heads of cherubim, designed by Donatello and executed by

The sacristy with the Cappella Rinuccini.

Desiderio da Settignano. A fine door designed by Giuliano da Maiano (1472) opens on one of the long sides of the rectangular interior. The ribbed dome and lantern are set above the walls articulated by pilasters. A door in the right-hand corner of the First Cloister, by Michelozzo or Benedetto da Maiano, opens into the **Second Cloister**, or *Large Cloister* designed by Brunelleschi and probably decorated by Rossellino. Entrance to the antique *Refectory* and the **Museum of the Works of Santa Croce**, is on the right of the first cloister.

MUSEUM OF THE WORKS OF SANTA CROCE - Installed next to the Church, the museum consists of six rooms situated in what used to be the convent. The entrance room contains a fine fresco, *Saint Francis distributing bread to the Friars*, by Jacopo Ligozzi. The door on the right leads into a large hall (the old **Refectory**) dominated by a large fresco by Taddeo Gaddi of the *Tree of Life*, a *Last Supper* and various *Episodes from the Life of Christ*. The room also contains Cimabue's famous *Crucifix*, heavily damaged during the flood in 1966.

Cimabue, Crucifix (ca. 1300), *Refectory.*

The De' Pazzi Chapel and, above, two Della Robbia roundels in the interior.

The profile of the soaring bell tower of the Badia Fiorentina (left) facing the squared-off, crenellated "Volognana Tower" of the Bargello (right).

CHURCH OF BADIA FIOREN-TINA
- The church of Badia, Benidictine, was founded before the 11th century but was completely reconstructed in the 17th century.

The **interior**, Greek-cross plan, contains a number of masterpieces of Renaissance sculpture: on the wall to the left of the entrance, the fine panel of the *Apparition of the Virgin to St. Bernard* (1480), is one of Filippino Lippi's finest works. Near the apse is the entrance to the **Small Cloister of the Aranci**, with a 14th-century fresco cycle of *Scenes from the life of St. Bernard* by an unknown painter.

PALAZZO DEL BARGELLO -
The Bargello palace looks like a fortress and has a powerful **crenellated tower** (the *Volognana*) above the severe façade. It was built in 1255, as the headquarters of the *Capitano del Popolo*; it then became the residence of the *podestà* and afterwards was used by the Council of Justice. From 1574, the Bargello (or Captain of Justice) resided here and it was then called with today's name. Since 1859, the palace has been the seat of the **National Museum** which contains Renaissance sculpture and masterpieces of the minor arts from various periods.

NATIONAL MUSEUM OF THE BARGELLO

The enormous **Entrance hall** is on pillars with solid vaulting, and has heraldic decorations on the walls with the coats of arms of the *podestà* (13th-14th century).

From here you enter the scenic **Courtyard**, irregular and original. The coats of arms of many *podestà* are here, as well as the picturesque insignia of the quarters and the districts into which the city was once divided, under the portico. The 16th-century statues, set against the walls, are by Bandinelli, Ammannati, Giambologna and Danti. On the same wall, there also are some pieces of the Medici armoury. The courtyard leads to a **Hall**, with a collection of 14th-century sculpture. In the Room close to the open staircase

there are important works by Michelangelo: the *Bacchus* (1496), an early work of great power and softness, the *Pitti Tondo,* with the *Madonna teaching Jesus and St. John to read* (1504), the *David* or *Apollo* (1530), and the *Brutus* (1540). There are also works by Ammannati, Giambologna (including his famous *Mercury* - 1564), Tribolo, Danti, Francavilla and Sansovino, who made a *Bacchus* of his own to compete with Michelangelo's.

The bronze *bust of Cosimo I* by Cellini, made for Portoferraio in Elba and brought back in 1781, is also in the

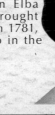

The inner portico and Giambologna's bronze Peacock *(1567).*

same room. The **Open staircase** leads to the **Loggia**, embellished by works by various 16th- century artists.

The first room to the right, once the Hall of the General Council, is now the **Donatello Room**, and contains many of his works such as the *St. George* (1416) with its composed energy, made for the niche in Orsanmichele; the young *St. John,* slender and mystical; the marble *David* (1408); and the bronze *David,* the first delicate Renaissance nude made around 1430. Also by Donatello, are the *Marzocco,* the symbol of the city, and the lively bronze *Amor-Attis,* revealing a classic influence.

In addition to works by Luca della Robbia, Ghiberti, Vecchietta and Agostino di Duccio, the room also contains the trial panels which Ghiberti and Brunelleschi made, in 1402, for the competition for the second door of the Florentine Baptistery (there were six participants). Ghiberti's relief succeeds in giving us a complete view of the story of the *Sacrifice of Isaac,* while Brunelleschi's panel, well articulated, gives the impression of a juxtaposition of parts.

Access to the **Collection of Decorative Arts**, mostly based on the donation of the Carrand Collections, is from the hall. Goldwork and enamels from the Middle Ages to the 16th century, seals and various metal objects are in the **Hall of the Podestà**. In the adjacent **Chapel of the Podestà**, where those condemned to death passed their last hours, there are Giottesque frescoes of *Paradise, Hell* and *Stories of the Saints.* This floor is completed by the **Hall of the Ivories**, with rare carvings dating from antiquity to the 15th century; the **Hall of the Goldwork**, with numerous works of sacred art,

Michelangelo, Bacchus (1497-99).

Sansovino, Bacchus (1520).

Michelangelo, Pitti Madonna (1504-08).

Benvenuto Cellini,
Mercury
(mid-16th C.).

and the **Hall of the Majolicas**. The second floor of the Bargello contains other rooms dedicated to great artists: the first, known as the **Giovanni della Robbia Room**, contains a number of the master's sculptures, including the predella with *Christ and Saints,* the *St. Dominic,* the *Pietà* and the *Annunciation.* The following **Andrea della Robbia Room** houses the *Madonna of the Architects* and other works in glazed terra-cotta.

In the **Verrocchio Room** are the *Resurrection,* the *bust of a young woman,* the *Madonna and Child,* the bronze *David,* and other works by the master, as well as various busts and sculptures by Mino da Fiesole, and the group of *Hercules and Antaeus* by Pollaiolo, a vibrating force of the two struggling figures. Other bronze sculptures are in the **Hall of the Bronzes** with the fireplace of Casa Borgherini by Benedetto da Rovezzano; the **Hall of the Arms** houses military vestments from the Middle Ages to the 17th century. The museum is completed by the **Hall of the Tower** with tapestries and the **Medici Medal show-case**, with works by artists such as Pisanello, Cellini, Michelozzo and others.

Michelangelo,
Brutus
(ca. 1540).

Luca della Robbia,
Madonna and Child
with Two Angels
(1450).

CHURCH OF ORSANMICHELE

The structure was once a loggia used as a communal granary which later became an oratory. Built by Arnolfo di Cambio in 1290, it was transformed between 1337 and 1404.

The **exterior** appears as a large cube with the arcades of the loggia at the base, closed by a delicate late Gothic marble decoration of elegant form; the upper part is more uniform with walls in "pietra forte" and two tiers of large mullioned windows with two lights.

A series of tabernacles and statues runs along the walls of the church. On the *via Calzaiuoli* are *St. John the Baptist* by Ghiberti (1414-16), the tabernacle by Donatello and Michelozzo with the group of the *Doubting Thomas* (1464-83) by Andrea del Verrocchio, and Giambologna's *St. Luke* (1601). On the *via Orsanmichele* are

St. Peter (1408-13) by Donatello, *St. Philip* (1405-10) by Nanni di Banco, the *Four crowned Saints* (1408) also by Nanni di Banco, and the *St. George* (1416) by Donatello (bronze copy of the marble original now in the Bargello Museum).

On the *via dell'Arte della Lana* are the *St. Matthew* (1420) by Ghiberti, the *St. Stephen* (1426-28) also by Ghiberti, and *St. Eligius* (1415) by Nanni di Banco. In the *via dei Lamberti* are *St. Mark* (1411-13) by Donatello, *St. James* by a pupil of Ghiberti, *Madonna and Child* (1399) attributed to Simone Talenti, and *St. John the Evangelist* by Baccio da Montelupo. The terracotta medallions are by the Della Robbia brothers.

Inside there are a series of frescoes and panels dedicated to the *Patron Saints* (14th-16th century). Over the altar is a marble group of *St. Anne, Virgin and Child* by Francesco da Sangallo. But the masterpiece, is the magnificent tabernacle by Orcagna (1355-59) in International Gothic style, and finely decorated with remarkable sculptures and mosaics. The panel framed by the **tabernacle** is by Bernardo Daddi.

PIAZZA DELLA REPUBBLICA - The present-day Piazza della Repubblica (formerly *Piazza Vittorio Emanuele II*) was once the heart of medieval Florence, and even earlier of Roman Florence. This was originally the

One of the elegant aediculae that decorate the exterior of Orsanmichele and a view of the church.

Piazza della Repubblica.

The Boar *of the fountain affectionately known as "il Porcellino".*

site of the Forum, the centre of the city's public and commercial life, where many centuries later the **Mercato Vecchio** established itself, conserving the mercantile vocation of the old Roman site. Around it was the Jewish quarter, or **Ghetto**, full of charming streets and alleys which numerous painters, including Telemaco Signorini, reproduced in drawings and canvases towards the end of the 19th century, shortly before it finally disappeared.

LOGGE DEL MERCATO NUOVO AND FOUNTAIN OF THE PORCELLINO - The Loggia del Mercato Nuovo is a basic structure on a square ground plan built by G. B. del Tasso (1547-51). A characteristic market of typically Florentine craft objects (straw, leather) is held here. On the south side of the loggia is Pietro Tacca's famous *Fountain of the Boar* (1639) later called *Porcellino* or Piglet by the Florentines.

The Logge del Mercato Nuovo.

PONTE VECCHIO

It is the city's oldest bridge, built, as it appears today, in 1345 by Neri di Fioravante, with its elegant structure on three arches. A characteristic feature of the bridge is the row of small houses on either side; in the 14th century, the features were much more regular, and as time passed they have aquired the picturesque variety, you can admire today. At the centre of the bridge, the buildings are interrupted, and an opening allows a fine view of the Arno and the other bridges. A bronze bust of *Benvenuto Cellini* by Raffaello Romanelli (1900) has here been placed. Above the houses, on the upstream side of the bridge, is the **Vasari Corridor**, built by Vasari for Cosimo I to go from Palazzo Pitti to Palazzo Vecchio. The shops on either side of the bridge are still working and are the workshops of artisan goldsmiths.

Ponte Vecchio with the Torre d'Arnolfo in the background. Above, the bust of Benvenuto Cellini.

A view of the Vasari Corridor above Ponte Vecchio.

The Santa Trinita bridge, Column of Justice and the façade of the church of Santa Trinita.

PONTE SANTA TRINITA - After Ponte Vecchio, this is considered the most beautiful bridge in the city. It was built by Bartolomeo Ammannati, with Michelangelo's suggestions. Fine statues are set at the entrances to the bridge: on the side towards the city, *Spring* by Pietro Francavilla is on the left, and *Summer* by Cacini is one the right. On the opposite side are *Autumn*, also by Cacini, and *Winter* by Taddeo Landini.

CHURCH OF SANTA TRINITA - The church already existed in the 11th century and was rebuilt and enlarged in the 13th and 14th centuries.
The **façade** is linear and decorated with a lovely stone medallion by Buontalenti (1593).
The **interior** is simple and severe, with a nave and two aisles separated by pillars. In the first chapel of the right aisle, stands out a fine 14th-century *Crucifix*; in the third, a *Madonna with Saints* by Neri di Bicci; in the fourth, the *Annunciation* by Lorenzo Monaco

Church of Santa Trinita: Ghirlandaio, Adoration of the Shepherds
(1485), Sassetti Chapel.

(1425), and in the fifth, a lovely
altar by Benedetto da Rovezzano. At the end of the crossing, there is the **Sacristy** and
then the **Sassetti Chapel**. The
fresco over the entrance arch
depicts the *Tiburtine Sibyl an-
nouncing the Birth of Christ to
Augustus;* inside, *Scenes from
the Life of St. Francis;* behind
the altar, the *Miracle of the Re-
suscitated Child;* above the altar, *St. Francis Receiving the
Rule from Pope Honorius,* all
by Ghirlandaio (1483-86). On
the walls are the *tombs of the
Sassetti family,* by Giuliano da
Sangallo and, on the altar, the
Adoration of the Shepherds, also by Ghirlandaio.

Next comes the **Major Chapel**,
with a triptych of the *Trinity
and Saints* by Mariotti di Nardo
(1416) on a 15th-century altar,
while parts of frescoes by
Alessio Baldovinetti are in the
vault. In the second chapel, is
the *tomb of the bishop of
Fiesole Benozzo Federici,* a
marveluous work by Luca della
Robbia (1454-56), decorated
with a charming frieze of painted and glazed terra-cotta tiles.
In the fifth chapel of the left
aisle, is a wooden statue of the
Magdalen begun by Desiderio
da Settignano (1464) and finished by Benedetto da Maiano
(1468). Also see in the third
chapel, the *Annunciation* by
Neri di Bicci and in the fouth
chapel, the *Coronation of the
Virgin,* probably by a pupil of
Neri (1491).

CHURCH OF SANTA MARIA NOVELLA

Begun in 1279, by Sisto da Firenze and Ristoro da Campi, it was finished in 1348, by Jacopo Talenti, with the bell tower in Romanesque Gothic style (1330).

The marvelous **façade** was remade between 1456 and 1470 by Leon Battista Alberti, who designed the portal and the wall above, divided into compartments by inlaid marble and framed by the coats of arms (heraldicsails) of the Rucellai, who commissioned the great work. Two large upside-down volutes join the sides with the centre divided by four engaged pilasters and closed by a triangular tympanum.

The **interior** is divided into a nave and two aisles by pillars carrying pointed vaults. A fine mosaic *Nativity* based on a cartoon by Filippo Lippi, is set over the central door. In the second bay of the **right aisle** is the *tomb of the Beata Villana*, by Rossellino (1451), and the **Chapel of the Pura**, a Renaissance structure built in honour of a miraculous *Madonna*, a 14th-century fresco, in the left-hand corner. In the right arm of the crossing is the terra-cotta *bust of St. Antonine* and, above, the *tomb of Tedice Aliotti, Bishop of Fiesole*, by Tino di Camaino. A flight of steps leads to the **Rucellai Chapel**, with remains of frescoes of the *Martyrdom of St. Catherine* by Giuliano Bugiardini; at the centre of the

Details of the façade and below, the adjacent wall of the old cemetery.

pavement is the fine *tombslab for Leonardo Dati* by Ghiberti (1423). From the crossing, there is the entrance to: the **Bardi Chapel**, with the *Madonna of the Rosary* by Vasari (1568), and remains of 14th-century frescoes; and the **Chapel of Filippo Strozzi the Elder**, with important frescoes, including scenes from the *Lives of St. Philip and St. John Evangelist* by Filippino Lippi (1503).

On the back wall there is the *tomb of Filippo Strozzi* by Benedetto da Maiano (1491). The **Cappella Maggiore of the Tornabuoni**, houses a fine bronze *Crucifix* by Giambologna on the altar, and frescoes on the vault and on the walls with scenes from the *Lives of St. John the Baptist* (on the right) and *of the Virgin* (on the left) by Domenico Ghirlandaio (late 15th century).

Cappellone degli Spagnoli. A detail of the cycle of frescoes by Andrea di Bonaiuto, Allegory of the Church Militant and Triumphant. *One of the many interesting details is the view of the Duomo without its marble facing, as the 1367 plan by Andrea di Bonaiuto and other masters would have had it.*

The **Gondi Chapel**, by Giuliano da Sangallo, has fragments of frescoes by 13th-century Greek painters, and on the back wall, the famous *Crucifix* by Brunelleschi; next come the **Gaddi Chapel** with the *Miracle of Jesus* by Bronzino on the altar; the **Chapel of the Strozzi family of Mantua**, displays frescoes of the *Last Judgement* on the back wall, *Hell* on the right, and *Paradise* on the left, by Nardo di Cione or by Orcagna. A large panel of the *Triumphant Christ* by Orcagna (1357), is on the altar. Next comes the **Sacristy**, built by Jacopo Talenti (1350); on the right, a marble lavabo in a glazed terra-cotta niche by Giovanni della Robbia (1498).

Masaccio's *Trinity,* an extremely important fresco, is in the **left aisle**; on the second pillar there is a *pulpit*, designed by Brunelleschi, with classical decorative elements, and bas-reliefs by Buggiano (1462).

The gate to the left of the façade leads to the Cloisters of the **Large Convent** (now used for civil and military purposes): the **First Cloister** is the oldest, it is in Romanesque style (1350), and the various frescoes with *scenes from the Old Testament* by Paolo Uccello, have been detached, and are now exposed in the refectory.

Nearby, is the famous **Spanish Chapel**, built by Jacopo Talenti (1359) in honour of St. Thomas of Aquinas: on the entrance wall are the scenes from the *Life of St. Peter Martyr* and above, in the vault, the *Ascension.* The side walls are decorated with allegories of the *Triumph of Wisdom and the Church Militant and Triumphant* by Andrea di Buonaiuto (1366-68). The so-called **Small Cloister of the Dead**, in

Romanesque style, and containing a number of *tomb slabs,* leads to the **Great Cloister**, the largest in the city, with over fifty arches, and completely frescoed by the greatest Florentine painters of the 15th and 16th centuries.

Cappellone degli Spagnoli. A cell of the vaulted ceiling.

MASACCIO
Trinità (1427)

The fresco was unknown to art historians until 1861, when the altar that Vasari had built there in the course of modifications in the church was demolished. It is certainly one of the most intense and significant paintings in all Florentine art of the Quattrocento. Replaced in its original position after a long restoration, the Trinità can now be admired in all its expressive vigour, which is built symmetrically according to a pyramidal arrangement of the figures within a Renaissance architectural structure whose perspective effect was suggested to Masaccio by Brunelleschi. At the top of the composition is God the Father, under whom the crucified Christ acts as a fulcrum for the entire composition: at the sides the figures of the Madonna and St John, at whose feet are the donors, members of the Lenzi family. Below them the composition ends with a skeleton on a sarcophagus, a symbol of the transience of human life, to which the inscription above also refers («Io fui già quel che voi siete e quel ch'io son voi anche sarete».)

CHURCH OF SAN LORENZO

Consecrated by St. Ambrose in 393, it is the oldest church of the city. It was rebuilt along Romanesque lines in 1060. The present building dates from 1423 and was designed and carried out by Brunelleschi. The simple bare **façade** lacks the marble covering; Michelangelo's design was never carried out. The **internal façade**, which Michelangelo also designed, is comprised of three doors between two pilasters with garlands of oak and laurel, and a balcony on two Corinthian columns.

The **interior** has a nave separated from the side aisles by Corinthian columns. The ceiling, in white-ground coffering has beautiful rose windows. The second chapel of the **right aisle**, contains the *Wedding of the Virgin* by Rosso Fiorentino (1523) with the bright colours, typical of the Mannerist painters; next to it is the Gothic *tomb slab of F. Landini,* organist, carved in 1398. After the

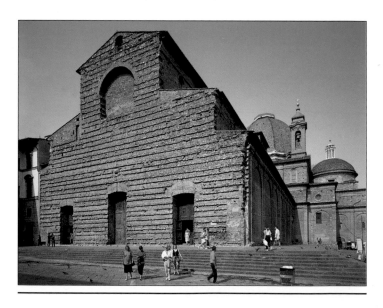

The interior of the church of San Lorenzo, and one of the two bronze pulpits by Donatello.

two paintings of *St. Lawrence* and the *Adoration of the Magi*, comes the ciborium, dating 1461, by Desiderio da Settignano.

In the right-hand chapel of the transept, there is a Roman *sarcophagus*, used to bury Niccolò Stenone; in the main chapel, is a marble *Crucifix* by Baccio da Montelupo, while the central **dome** is frescoed with *Florentine Saints in Glory* by Vincenzo Meucci (1742). The left transept contains the wooden statue of the *Madonna and Child*, a polychrome late 14th-century work; the painting of *Saints* by the school of Ghirlandaio, and Filippo Lippi's *Annunciation* dip-

tych. The Annunciation dates from 1440, and has a remarkable feeling for space, due to the figures in third dimension and the perspective sudy of the building in the background. The **left aisle** contains the large fresco of the *Martyrdom of St. Lawrence* by Bronzino (1565-1569), and the marble choir, which may have been designed by Donatello. Under the arches of the last two bays of the nave, there are Donatello's two bronze *pulpits*, similar to two large classic arches on columns.

The Dionysiac scenes which fill in the empty spaces recall ancient monuments. The panels painted by Donatello's pupils – Bellano and Bertoldo – include the *Crucifixion,* the *Deposition,* part of the *Passion of Christ, St. John the Evangelist,* and the *Flagellation* on the left pulpit, and the *Martyrdom of St. Lawrence,* the *Resurrection,* and the other part of the *Passion* on the right pulpit.

The **Old Sacristy**, at the back of the left transept, was built by Brunelleschi, between 1419 and 1428. Built before the church, the sacristy is the first example of Renaissance architecture, and of the work of Brunelleschi, in Florence. A dome covers the square room, and a square apse opens off one wall. The structural lines are stressed by stone molding. Eight tondos by Donatello (1435-1443) with the *Four Evangelists* and *Scenes from the Life of St. John* are set into the corner pendentives and on the walls. The bronze doors and the stucco reliefs over the doors are also by Donatello, while the *funeral monument to Piero and Giovanni de' Medici* (1472) is by Andrea del Verrocchio. Andrea Cavalcanti made the balustrade of the apse, on a design by Donatello, as well as the *sarcophagus of Giovanni Bicci de' Medici and his wife.* On the opposite side, near the right transept of the church, there is the New Sacristy with the entrance from outside.

MEDICI CHAPELS - This big complex containing the Medici family tombs, is attached to the back of the Church of St. Lorenzo and it includes the underground quarters and various other rooms of the church.

The entrance is on the *Piazza Madonna degli Aldobrandini* and it leads to a vast and low hall, designed by Bountalenti, in which the visitor can admire the *tomb of Cosimo the Elder,* the one of *Donatello,* and of the various members of the *House of Lorraine,* as well as other grand-ducal sepulchers. From here one moves up to the **Cappella dei Principi** in part by Nigetti (Buontalenti also worked on the design), dating from 1602, and finished in the 18th century. From the outside, the building is Baroque, with a high drum, and big windows, supporting a large dome faced in brick, similar to the dome on the cathedral.

The **interior** is octagonal in plan, entirely lined with semiprecious stones and marble in Baroque style. The base is decorated with the *16 coats of arms* of the Tuscan grand-ducal cities. Above are the six *coffers or tombs* of the Grand Dukes *Cosimo III, Francesco I, Cosimo I, Ferdinando I, Cosimo II, Ferdinando II,* over two of which stand *statues of the Grand Dukes* by Tacca. Narrow rooms open off from either side of the al-

The tomb of Giuliano, Duke of Nemours.

The dome of the Cappella dei Principi.

tar. Once sacristies, they now contain a collection of relics and the *treasure* which includes glass vases, church furniture and reliquaries dating from the 17th and 18th centuries.

A corridor leads from the Princes Chapel to the **New Sacristy**. This room, designed by Michelangelo around 1520, reverses the restrained balance of Brunelleschi's room in St. Lorenzo (Old Sacristy) in a dynamic concise series of wall decorations. Under the dome, with its perspective coffering, the walls of the square space have niches, pilasters and molding. Facing the tomb with the altar designed by Michelangelo, there is the *sarcophagus of Lorenzo the Magnificent and Giuliano de' Medici,* surmounted by statues of *St. Damian* (by Raffaello di Montelupo), the *Madonna and Child* (by Michelangelo) and *St. Cosmas* (by Giovannangelo Montorsoli). The *tombs of Giuliano, duke of Nemours,* and of *Lorenzo, duke of Urbino,* face each other at the centre of the other two walls. Michelangelo placed the sarcophaguses with the *Allegories of Time* under the statues of the dukes set in niches: Giuliano's tomb is watched over by *Day* and *Night,* while *Dusk* and *Dawn*

Michelangelo's tomb of Lorenzo, Duke of Urbino and, top, Dusk.

Michelangelo, the statue of Giuliano de' Medici, Duke of Nemours, and, top, Day. *Below, the Chapel of the Princes.*

watch over Lorenzo's. The accurate anatomical depiction of the figures, which are in part unfinished, expresses the intrinsic meaning through exterior form, and here Michelangelo created one of his greatest masterpieces.

ACADEMY GALLERY
(GALLERIA DELL'ACCADEMIA)

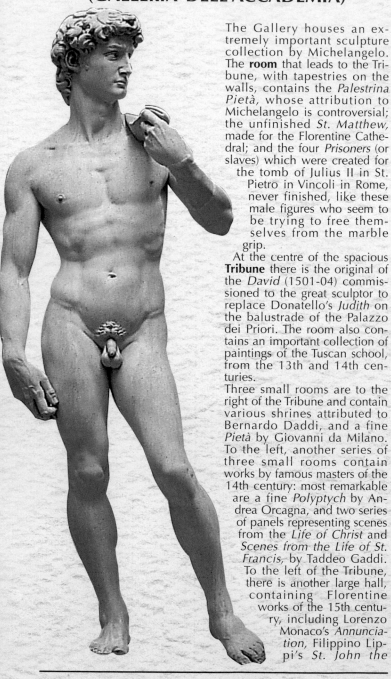

The Gallery houses an extremely important sculpture collection by Michelangelo. The **room** that leads to the Tribune, with tapestries on the walls, contains the *Palestrina Pietà*, whose attribution to Michelangelo is controversial; the unfinished *St. Matthew*, made for the Florentine Cathedral; and the four *Prisoners* (or slaves) which were created for the tomb of Julius II in St. Pietro in Vincoli in Rome, never finished, like these male figures who seem to be trying to free themselves from the marble grip.

At the centre of the spacious **Tribune** there is the original of the *David* (1501-04) commissioned to the great sculptor to replace Donatello's *Judith* on the balustrade of the Palazzo dei Priori. The room also contains an important collection of paintings of the Tuscan school, from the 13th and 14th centuries.

Three small rooms are to the right of the Tribune and contain various shrines attributed to Bernardo Daddi, and a fine *Pietà* by Giovanni da Milano. To the left, another series of three small rooms contain works by famous masters of the 14th century: most remarkable are a fine *Polyptych* by Andrea Orcagna, and two series of panels representing scenes from the *Life of Christ* and *Scenes from the Life of St. Francis*, by Taddeo Gaddi. To the left of the Tribune, there is another large hall, containing Florentine works of the 15th century, including Lorenzo Monaco's *Annunciation*, Filippino Lippi's *St. John the*

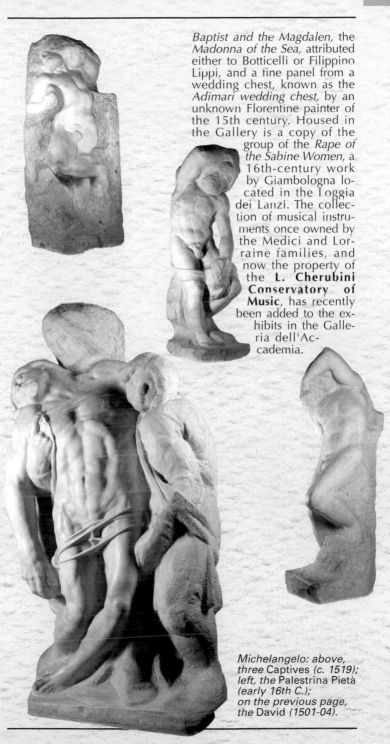

Baptist and the Magdalen, the *Madonna of the Sea,* attributed either to Botticelli or Filippino Lippi, and a fine panel from a wedding chest, known as the *Adimari wedding chest,* by an unknown Florentine painter of the 15th century. Housed in the Gallery is a copy of the group of the *Rape of the Sabine Women,* a 16th-century work by Giambologna located in the Loggia dei Lanzi. The collection of musical instruments once owned by the Medici and Lorraine families, and now the property of the **L. Cherubini Conservatory of Music**, has recently been added to the exhibits in the Galleria dell'Accademia.

Michelangelo: above, three Captives *(c. 1519); left, the* Palestrina Pietà *(early 16th C.); on the previous page, the* David *(1501-04).*

Beato Angelico,
Crucifixion *(15th C.).*

CHURCH AND CONVENT OF ST. MARCO - The Convent has been known since the 12th century. In 1437, Cosimo the Elder commissioned Michelozzo to restructure it, therefore it is the first convent built in the elegant simple forms of the Renaissance. The fine **Cloister** has a simple stone structure with brick cornices. Light arcades delimit the space on the ground floor. On the first floor are fine lunettes frescoed by Poccetti, Rosselli, Coccapani, Vanni, Cerrini, Dandini and other famous artists. But most of the frescoes in the cloister

are by Fra' Angelico, who passed the greater part of his life within these walls; his works include: *Crucifixion with St. Dominic* at the entrance to the cloister and the lunette over the door with *St. Peter Martyr.* A staircase leads to the next floor, with Fra' Angelico's famous *Annunciation* at the top; off the corridor is the splendid **Library**, by Michelozzo, and at the end of the corridor, **Cosimo's Cell** with a *Crucifix* in the ante-chamber and an *Adoration of the Magi* in the cell, both by Fra' Angelico. In the left corridor, you can admire an *Enthroned Madonna between Saints*, and in the cells that open off the corridor, other lovely works, all by Fra' Angelico: the *Annunciation,* the *Transfiguration, Christ in the Praetorium,* the *Marys at the Tomb,* the *Coronation,* the *Presentation in the Temple.* At the end of the corridor is **Savonarola's Cell**, with a portrait of the martyr painted by Fra' Bartolomeo. A flight of stairs on the right leads down to the **Small Refectory**, with a large fresco of the *Last Supper* by Ghirlandaio.

The **Hall of the Hospice** contains a number of panel paintings: the most remarkable are Fra' Angelico's *Last Judgement* and *Deposition*. The **Church** was restored in 1437 by Michelozzo himself; it was later remodeled by Giambologna (1580) and then by Silvani; the simple façade was redone between 1777 and 1780. The **interior** is linear and the carved and gilded ceiling is remarkable. Nearby is the **Chapel of St. Antoninus**, with marble and bronze decorations by Giambologna and Francavilla, and other works by Alessandro Allori and Battista Naldini; the frescoes in the dome are by Poccetti. To the left of the presbytery see the lovely **Chapel of the Sacrament**, decorated with frescoes by Poccetti and canvases by Santi di Tito, Passignano and Empoli.

CHURCH OF SS. ANNUNZIATA - When it was originally built (1250), outside the second circle of walls, it was an oratory. As time passed, the church was enlarged to the present size. Entrance to the church is through the so-called **Small Chapel of the Vows**, built by Antonio Manetti from designs by Michelozzo (1447). The space is remarkably scenic with lunettes frescoed with scenes from the *Life of the Virgin* (right wall), and outstanding works such as the *Assumption* (1513) by Rosso Fiorentino, the *Visitation* (1513) by Pontormo, the *Marriage of the Virgin* (1513), the *Birth of the Virgin* and the *Voyage of the Magi* (1511) by Andrea del Sarto. The small cloister is also decorated with *Scenes from the Life of St. Filippo Benizzi* by Cosimo Rosselli; and the *Punishment of the Blasphemers*, the *Healing of a Woman Possessed,* the *Resurrection of a Child,* the *Healing of a Child,* by Andrea del Sarto.

The **interior**, restructured in the middle of the 17th century, consists of a single great nave with arches, set between pilaster stips, that lead to the chapels on either sides; the church is enriched by the magnificent coffered ceiling by Volterrano (1664). The large tribune of the choir, with a hemispherical cupola designed by Leon Battista Alberti (1444), is

The portico in front of the facade of the church of Santissima Annunziata.

The Tabernacle of the Annunziata and the Loggiato dei Serviti.

the **Giambologna Chapel** transformed by the sculptor for his own burial (1598). Michelozzo's terra-cotta statue of *John the Baptist* is at the back of the left transept; the fourth chapel of the left side, is decorated with an *Assumption* by Perugino, while the first two chapels contain important frescoes by Andrea del Castagno – *Christ with St. Julian* and the *Trinity with St. Jerome between the Madonna and Mary of Cleofa*. A door from the left arm of the transept leads to the **Cloister of the Dead**, designed by Michelozzo (1453), and decorated with a fresco cycle of the *History* of *the Order of the Servi*, attributed to Bernardino Poccetti; the series is interrupted in the arch of the church portal, by Andrea del Sarto's *Madonna del Sacco* (1525). On the wall facing the side of the church see the *tomb of Guglielmo di Narbona*,

also particularly fine. To the left of the entrance, is the **Tabernacle of the Annunciata** by Michelozzo, built around a 14th-century fresco of the *Annunciation* traditionally considered miraculous. Near the presbytery, in the centre, there is

which represents the battle disposition of a knight from the 13th century.

GALLERY OF THE SPEDALE DEGLI INNOCENTI

The five rooms of this small museum contain important works of the 15th and 16th centuries, including the splendid *Adoration of the Christ Child,* with the sweet serene figures of the worshippers, by Ghirlandaio (1488), the terra-cotta *Madonna and Child* (1488) by Luca della Robbia; the famous *Madonna and Child with St. John* (1460) by Botticelli; and an imposing *Madonna and Saints* by Pietro di Cosimo.

SPEDALE DEGLI INNOCENTI

(Foundling Home) - Designed by Brunelleschi, the building was finished by Francesco Luna (1445). A lovely portico runs along the **façade**.
Its nine arcades are decorated with polychrome terra-cotta roundels with *Infants in Swaddling Clothes* (to remember that once this place gave hospitality to the orphans), by Andrea della Robbia (1463). Inside is a lovely courtyard and on the first floor there is a collection of detached frescoes and a Picture-gallery.

ARCHAEOLOGICAL MUSEUM

- It is one of the most important museums of this kind in Italy for the richness of its collections, which include examples of Egyptian, Etruscan, Greek and Roman antiquities.

Piazza SS. Annunziata: the equestrian statue of Grand Duke Ferdinand I, one of the two fountains by Tacca.
The Chimera, *one of the most celebrated Etruscan bronzes conserved at the Archaeological Museum.*

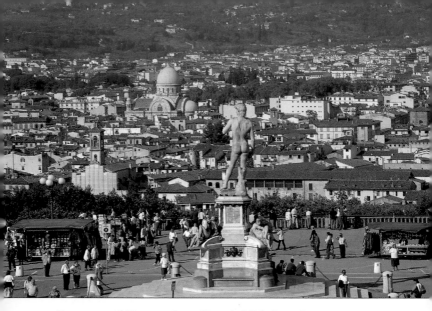

Panorama of Florence from Piazzale Michelangelo; below, Forte di Belvedere.

VIALE DEI COLLI AND PIAZZALE MICHELANGELO - The **Viale dei Colli** (Hill Avenue) winds for about six kilometres on the heights around the south side of the city, providing spots with fascinating views. It was laid out in 1868, by the architect Giuseppe Poggi, who also made the plans for the **Piazzale Michelangelo**, an enormous terrace overlooking Flo-rence. In the piazzale are copies of Michelangelo's sculptures: *David* and the four *allegorical figures* on the Medici tombs in the New Sacristy of San Lorenzo. In the background, set above the piazzale, is the **Palazzina del Caffè** (1873), also by Poggi, which partly hides the churches of St. Salvatore and St. Miniato al Monte.

FORTE DI BELVEDERE - The Forte di Belvedere, or *of St. George*, was commissioned to Buontalenti (1590-95) by Ferdinando I. The building, set on a hilltop south of the Arno, dominates the city and the river from within its star-shaped fortified walls. The protected access is through an entrance hall and reaches the terrace in front of the **Palazzetto**, which is now used for exhibitions and art happenings. An opening in the bastions communicates with the **Boboli Gardens** below.

CHURCH OF SAN MINIATO AL MONTE

The Church of San Miniato al Monte, which was built as a chapel in the 4th century, owes its present structure to Bishop Hildebrand (1018). The lower part of the façade is decorated with fine arches; the upper part is simpler and has a fine 12th-century mosaic with *Christ between the Madonna and St. Miniato*.

The **inside** is tripartite, with a trussed timber ceiling. The inlaid marble pavement, with *signs of the zodiac* and *symbolic animals*, is of particular interest. On the walls are fragments of 13th- and 14th-century frescoes. The large **Crypt** is closed by a wrought-iron gate dating from 1338. The altar (11th cent.) preserves the bones of St. Miniato; fragments of frescoes by Taddeo Gaddi (1341) are on the vault. Returning from the crypt, see the raised **Presbytery**, which has a fine *pulpit* (1207) and inlaid wooden choir stalls. In the conch of the apse is a large

mosaic of *Christ between Mary and St. Miniato* (1277). To the right of the presbytery there is the entrance to the **Sacristy**, completely frescoed by Spinello Aretino (1387) with sixteen *Scenes from the Legend of St. Benedict*. Descending on the left of the presbytery, one arrives at the **Chapel of St. Jacopo**, known as the *Chapel of*

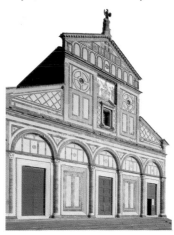

The large mosiac in the apse of the church of San Miniato al Monte and, below, the frescoes by Spinello Aretino in the sacristy.

the Cardinal of Portugal, designed by Antonio Manetti and decorated with five marvelous tondos by Luca della Robbia with the *Holy Spirit* and the *Four Cardinal Virtues*. The painting over the altar is a copy of a painting by Pietro del Pollaiolo, now in the Uffizi. At the centre of the church is the **Chapel of the Crucifix**, designed by Michelozzo, with a delicate glazed vault by Luca della Robbia.

PALAZZO PITTI

It is the most imposing of the city palaces, and dates from 1457 on a probable design by Brunelleschi; in the 16th century the Medici commissioned Ammannati to enlarge it.

The **façade**, 205 metres long and 36 metres high, consists of rusticated ashlars with some of the single blocks over two metres long. The only decorative elements are the *crowned heads of lions* between the ground floor window brackets.

Access to the **interior** is through the great portal with its central arch leading into a charming Doric atrium by Pasquale Poccianti (1850). This leads to Ammannati's famous courtyard, at the back of which is the *Grotto of Moses,* carved in porphyry by Raffaelle Curradi; antique Roman statues are set under the arcades at the sides, while to the right is the **Chapel** frescoed by Ademollo, with a magnificent mosaic altar and a fine *Crucifix* by Giambologna.

The grand staircase, lined with antique busts, begins on the same side of the courtyard; on the landing is the *Medici Genius* by Giambologna; the first floor goes to the vestibule of the **Royal Quarters** and the **Palatine Gallery**. On the second floor is the **Gallery of Modern Art**.

The portico in the right wing of the façade of the palace leads to the **Bacchus Courtyard**, today's main entrance to the Palatine Gallery and the **Museum of Silverware** with the *Fountain of Bacchus* by Cioli, which portrays the court dwarf of Cosimo I.

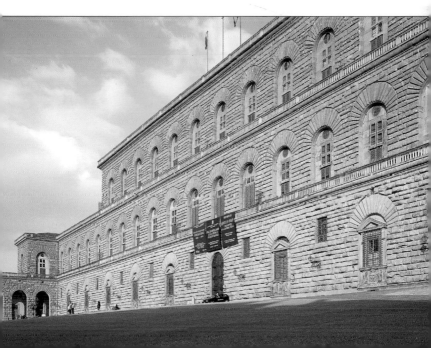

The Palatine Gallery is the second museum in the city, both for size and interest, after the Uffizi, and contains works of art extremely important for the history of art. It was realised by Ferdinando II de' Medici who commissioned Pietro da Cortona to decorate various rooms of the Gallery.

As time passed, the collection – a typically 17th-century *picture gallery* with the walls entirely covered with pictures in the fashion of the times – was enlarged by Cardinal Leopoldo de' Medici and, later, by the last members of the Medici family and by the Lorraine Grand Dukes. The Gallery consists of a series of rooms dedicated to gods and mythological figures, represented in the decoration.

Raphael, Madonna of the Chair *(1515).*

GALLERIA PALATINA

The Gallery houses numerous works which are a fine representation of the entire artistic panorama between the 15th and 18th centuries. Particularly important is the nucleus formed by the paintings of Titian, such as *The Concert*, and Raphael, by whom there are splendid portraits such as *The Veiled Woman*, *Maddalena Doni* and *'La Gravida'* alongside religious subjects like the *Madonna of the Grand-duke*, the *Madonna of the Chair*, the *Madonna 'dell'Impannata'* and the *Vision of Ezekiel.* The Florentine school is represented by Filippo Lippi (*Madonna and Child*) and by Andrea del Sarto (*Assumption with Apostles and Saints, Holy Family and Stories of Joseph*). There are also important works of 17th-century Italian art like the *Sleeping Cupid* by Caravaggio, and of North European art represented by paintings by Rubens, including *The Four Philosophers* and *The Consequences of War.*

Filippo Lippi, Madonna and Child *(ca. 1452).*

Raphael, The Veiled Woman *(1516).*

Raphael, Madonna of the Grand-duke *(1504-05).*

Titian, The Concert *(1510-13).*

Caravaggio,
Sleeping Cupid
(1606).

Pieter Paul Rubens,
The Four
Philosophers
(1606).

MODERN ART GALLERY - Situated on the second floor of Palazzo Pitti, it consists of over 2000 works of sculpture and painting by artists active between the beginning of the 19th century up to the early decades of the 20th century. The Gallery covers many rooms: the first of these contain works in neoclassic and Romantic style, with imposing historical paintings. **Rooms XXIII** and **XXIV** contain a rich collection of works by the most important Macchiaioli painters. Room XXIII contains some of the outstanding works by the father of the Macchiaioli movement, Giovanni Fattori.

BOBOLI GARDENS - The Boboli Gardens comprise the largest monumental green space in Florence. The history of the gardens goes back four centuries. In 1549, Cosimo I de' Medici commissioned them to Niccolò Pericoli, called Tribolo. After his death the work was continued and modified by Ammannati, Buontalenti, and finally Alfonso Parigi the Younger.

Today, entrance to the gardens is through the **Bacchus Courtyard**, beyond which is the charming **Buontalenti Grotto** (1583), an artificial grotto consisting of various chambers covered with artificial incrustations and frescoes. The fine alley flanked by Roman statues, leads to the **Amphitheater**, designed by Tribolo, at the centre of which is a large Roman *marble basin* and an Egyptian *obelisk* from Thebes (2nd cent. BC). The two Roman *statues* of *Septimius Severus* and a *Magistrate* near the Amphitheater are particularly fine. Further up, is a large basin called **Neptune's Pond** with a fine bronze *statue* of Neptune by Stoldo Lorenzi (1565) at the centre. On the highest level, at the back of the park, you can admire the *Statue of Abundance,* begun by Giambologna and finished by Tacca (1636).

Nearby are the old walls, constructed by Michelangelo in 1529, near a bastion with the **Grand Duke's Casino** and the nearby **Garden of the Knight** with the fine *Monkey fountain* by Pietro Tacca. Further downhill is an annex of Palazzo Pitti called the **Meridiana**, a pleasant neo-Gothic building (1832). An alternative itinerary from Neptune's Pond begins from a steep alley, known as the *Viottolone*, which leads to the *Piazzale dell'Isolotto*. Here, at the centre of a charming garden, is the stupendous *Oceanus Fountain* by Giambologna.

The **Palazzina del Cavaliere** hosts the **Museo delle Porcellane**, with its magnificent collection of porcelains from Sèvres, Chantilly, Vienna, Meissen, Worcester, and other centers of production.

Buontalenti's Grotto.

CHURCH OF SANTO SPIRITO
- The church of Santo Spirito, founded in 1250, received its present form in the 15th century, when it was built from a model by Brunelleschi, who had conceived it as a twin to the church of St. Lorenzo. The **façade**, however, was never finished, and is still only a rough plastered wall with an undefined silhouette at the top. The fine **dome** was designed by Brunelleschi, while the soaring **Bell tower** is by Baccio d'Agnolo (1503).

The **interior** is one of the finest examples of Renaissance architecture, a Latin-cross with three spacious aisles. The colonnade moves forward in a succession of light arches, supported by 35 elegant Corinthian columns in *pietra serena,* forming an internal portico. The ground plan of the 40 semicircular chapels repeats the semicircular rhythm of the arches.

The **internal façade** is comprised of three large doors and was made by Salvi d'Andrea (1483) on Brunelleschi's design. Behind the high altar is a *Crucifix* that may be an early work by Michelangelo.

Entry to the **Vestibule**, by Giuliano da Sangallo and Cronaca, and to the Sacristy is near the organ. The **Sacristy** has a fine octagonal ground plan by Giuliano da Sangallo. The Vestibule leads to the **First Cloister**, in 17th-century style, with frescoes of the same period. Then comes the **Second Cloister**, built by Ammannati and frescoed by Poccetti (the cloister is not at present open to the public since it is occupied by the recruiting centre). Entry to the nearby **Refectory** is from the square. It contains the imposing fresco of the *Last Supper* by Nardo di Cione.

CHURCH OF ST. MARIA DEL CARMINE
- The 14th-century building was almost completely destroyed in a fire in 1771. The present structure is therefore 18th-century and was built by G. Ruggeri and G. Mannaioni on a Latin-cross plan with a single aisle. The works **inside** include Vasari's *Crucifixion* on the third altar to the right. One of the greatest works of the entire Renaissance came through the fire miraculously intact – the **Brancacci Chapel** in the right transept preserves a cycle of extremely important frescoes which have recently been restored. The frescoes were begun in 1425 by Masolino da Panicale, who painted the *Temptation of Adam and Eve*, in the first compartment above right, *St. Peter Resuscitating Tabitha*, in the first scene to the right of the large compart-

The clean lines of the facade of the church of Santo Spirito.

The facade and the interior of the church of St. Maria del Carmine.

with *St. Peter Baptizing the Neophytes* and the splendid *Expulsion from Paradise*, in the first panel above left. Masaccio then went on to the large compartment at the top of the left wall, with *St. Peter taking the Coin from the Mouth of the Fish* (left), *Jesus Ordering Peter to Fish* (center), and *St. Peter paying the Tribute to the Publican* (right). In the lower tier, the compartment to the right of the altar with *St. Peter and St. John distributing the Goods* and the *Death of Ananias* by Masaccio, as also, to the left of the altar, *St. Peter Healing the Sick with his Shadow;* on the lower part of the left wall, *St. Peter in Cattedra* and part of *St. Peter*

ment at the top, and the *Preaching of St. Peter* above, to the left of the altar. The compartment on the right wall, *St. Peter Heals a Cripple*, is in part by the great Masaccio, who also painted the compartment above to the right of the altar,

Bringing back to Life the Son of the Prefect Theophilus of Antioch. Finally, the last compartment of the left wall, *St. Peter in Prison Visited by St. Paul,* in the lower part of the right wall, the *Angel Freeing St. Peter from Prison* and the double scene of *St. Peter before the Prefect Agrippa* and the *Crucifixion of St. Peter* are by another great artist, Filippino Lippi.

Cappella Brancacci: Masolino, Healing of the Lame Man and the Resurrection of Tabitha *(1425).*

MASACCIO
Tribute Money (1426)

The fresco refers to the episode of the Gospel in which Christ and the Apostles are stopped by a tax-collector who asks them for tribute money. Christ, respectful of earthly laws, shows Peter a lake where he will find a fish with the money in its mouth to be given to the tax-collector. The Tribute Money is the first monumental scene of Renaissance painting, the supreme expression of the results of Massaccio's research into perspective and his meticulous study of the psychological dimension of portraiture. The volumetric and syntactical characteristics of the group are in fact intrinsically linked to define the content of the story and the evocative quality of the scene. The human figures simultaneously determine their own inner space by means of an intense expressive charge and give meaning to the surrounding space whose perspective scheme they themselves coordinate. The serene face of Christ, to which the almost adolescent and classically measured figure of St John shows the closest resemblance, is the narrative centre and compositional fulcrum of the scene. Around Christ the anxious expressions of the assembled Apostles convey their expectancy of the miracle, on which they confer all the importance and solemnity due to it as a key event in the great Christian epos.

GUIDE TO THE ARTISTS

ALBERTI Leon Battista
(1404-1472)
Architect and Humanist. A multi-talented humanist, architect, treatise-writer, poet and author of dialogues in Latin and the vernacular, Alberti studied in Genoa, Padua and Bologna, and lived for a long time in Rome, although it is with Florence that his name is most closely linked. Here he distinguished himself as a skilled draughtsman and innovative user of perspective, knew and admired Brunelleschi, Masaccio and Donatello, glorified in the preamble of his celebrated treatise *Della Pittura*, and here particularly he conceived illustrious creations like Palazzo Rucellai, the facade of Santa Maria Novella, the tribune of Santissima Annunziata, almost practical applications of the theories expounded in his most important and influential work, *De Re Aedificatoria*.

AMMANNATI Bartolomeo
(1511-1592)
Architect and Sculptor. After training as a sculptor at the school of Jacopo Sansovino, Ammannati began his career as an architect at the court of Julius II in Rome. Returning to Florence, for Cosimo I De' Medici he planned and carried out the enlargement of the original Palazzo Pitti, building the grandiose and solemn courtyard. This was followed by the Ponte Santa Trinita and the monumental Fountain of Neptune in Piazza Signoria, illustrious works that made him one of the most typical representatives of late Tusco-Roman Mannerism.

ARNOLFO DI CAMBIO
(1245-1302)
Born in Colle Val d'Elsa and trained in the school of Nicola Pisano, Arnolfo was a talented sculptor and architect. After having worked in Bologna and Siena he moved to Rome where he lived for many years. Here he perfected his art, succeeding in

blending austere classical forms with the decorative motifs of Cosmatesque art, as numerous masterpieces testify. Returning to Florence in 1296, he distinguished himself as an architect, working on the most prestigious building projects: Santa Maria del Fiore, the Badia, Santa Croce and Palazzo Vecchio.

BEATO ANGELICO (1400-1455)
Born in Vicchio del Mugello, Guidolino di Pietro became a Dominican monk with the name of Fra Giovanni da Fiesole around 1418, but went down in history for his exceptional pictorial skills as Beato ('the blessed') Angelico. His works, in which the search for pure luminous tones is combined with a figurative style clearly influenced by the models of Brunelleschi and Masaccio, still ennoble numerous rooms of the convent of San Marco, now a museum.

BOTTICELLI (1445-1510)
Painter. The Florentine artist Sandro Filipepi, known as Botticelli, trained as a painter in the workshops of Filippo Lippi and Verrocchio before opening one of his own that soon attracted the attention of contemporary high society. Protected by Lorenzo Il Magnifico and closely connected with the humanists of the Medici court, he developed a mysticism and philosophy that profoundly influenced all his art, distinguished by spiritual intensity and a deeply communicative chromatic brilliance. The allegories and classical myths of his early works were replaced in time with religious themes, previously heralded by the frescoes of the Sistine Chapel executed between 1481 and 1482 which marked the final act of Florentine Humanism.

BRUNELLESCHI Filippo
(1377-1446)
Florentine sculptor and goldsmith, but above all the unri-

valled master of an architecture imbued with a new classicism and a successful application of the laws of perspective. Brunelleschi travelled widely and carried out meticulous technical studies in Rome before engaging in that prodigious activity which between 1419 and 1446 blossomed in Florence in a whole series of splendid masterpieces: the Spedale degli Innocenti, San Lorenzo, the Pazzi Chapel, the Palagio di Parte Guelfa, Santo Spirito and the cupola of Santa Maria del Fiore, the cathedral where he had the honour, as the only layman, of being buried.

BUONTALENTI Bernardo
(1503-1572)
Architect and Sculptor. One of the most active and esteemed sculptors and architects of Florentine Mannerism, Buontalenti's name is associated mainly with the Casino di San Marco, the facade of Santa Trinita and Forte di Belvedere. He was also responsible for an elaborate design for the plan of the city of Livorno and the apparatuses for festivities and performances organized by the grand-ducal family, many drawings of which are now kept at the Uffizi.

CELLINI Benvenuto (1500-1571)
Goldsmith and Sculptor. After training in the workshop of a Florentine goldsmith, Cellini was several times forced to leave the city after being involved in brawls and other violent episodes. He fled first of all to Siena, then to Rome, where he participated actively in the defence of Castel Sant'Angelo during the siege of 1527 and where he worked and was protected by Pope Clement VII and his successor Paul III, and subsequently moved to the court of Francis I in France. Returning to Florence in 1545, he was hired by Cosimo I De' Medici, to for whom he offered numerous examples of his excellent skill as a goldsmith and

sculptor. For the Grand-duke he made, among other things, the elaborate and majestic statue of *Perseus*. In the final years of his life he demonstrated a certain literary talent, devoting himself between 1558 and 1566 to the writing of his autobiography.

CIMABUE (1240-1302)

The work of Bencivieni di Pepo, or Benvenuto di Giuseppe, the Florentine painter known as Cimabue, was characterized by a balanced plasticism and intense passion that marked a breaking away from conventional Byzantine iconographies. Active in Rome in 1272, and in Arezzo and Assisi, where he frescoed the transept of the Upper Basilica, he later executed the absidal mosaic of Pisa cathedral before dedicating himself to the fabric of the cathedral of Santa Maria del Fiore in Florence.

DELLA ROBBIA

A veritable dynasty of sculptors, the Della Robbia family - Luca (1400-1482), his nephew Andrea (1435-1525) and the latter's son Giovanni (1469-1529) - with their Florentine workshop were responsible for the production of characteristic ivory-white and light-blue enamelled terracotta. The expressive force and refined elegance of their works can be admired today in the Duomo, the Spedale degli Innocenti and in Santa Maria Novella, and betrays at times, especially in the case of Luca, the discernible influences of illustrious masters, particularly Ghiberti and Donatello.

DONATELLO (1386-1466)

Donato di Niccolò Bardi, known as Donatello, was born and grew up in Florence, first as a workshop boy, then as an assistant of Ghiberti, and lastly as a close friend of Brunelleschi and Michelozzo. Summoned to work for the Opera del Duomo as early as 1408, he soon distinguished himself for the vigorous plasticism and the intense refined expressiveness of his sculptures. His

work was requested to embellish the Duomo, the Campanile, Orsanmichele and San Lorenzo, and was greatly admired even outside Florence, in Rome and particularly in Padua, where the artist stayed for long periods.

GHIBERTI Lorenzo (1378-1455)

Florentine, sculptor of reliefs par excellence, architect, painter, skilled goldsmith and author of the unfinished but highly esteemed Commentaries, Ghiberti came to the fore when he won the competition held in 1401 for the second door of the Baptistery. He worked on the twenty-eight panels for two decades, a period in which he also produced other fine works for the Duomo and the church of Orsanmichele. In 1425, again for the Baptistery, he started what would become for its spectacular effects and preciosity of style his masterpiece, the famous Gate of Paradise.

GHIRLANDAIO Domenico (1449-1494)

Domenico Bigordi, known as Ghirlandaio, was born in Florence and although being apprenticed as a painter in the workshop of Verrocchio was inspired in his youth by Domenico Veneziano and Alessio Baldovinetti. But when in 1481 he participated in the decoration of the Sistine Chapel he displayed what would later become the particular characteristics of his art: a vivid realism, a clear descriptive tendency and the presence in his frescoes of celebrated contemporary figures, characteristics which reappeared in the great Florentine cycles of Santa Maria Novella and Santa Trinita and made him one of the most celebrated and admired painters of his time.

GIAMBOLOGNA (1529-1608)

Sculptor. A sculptor of Flemish origin, Jean de Boulogne came to Italy in 1550 and, after a stay in Rome studying classical sculptures and the works of Michelangelo, settled in Florence where his services were hired by the

Medici family. His output was extremely varied: from the equestrian monuments of the Grand-dukes to elaborate fountains, including that of Neptune in Bologna, a grandiose work in its overall composition as well as in the smallest details of dolphins, cherubs and mermaids surrounding the god, and sculptural decorations for the gardens of many Florentine villas and the Boboli Gardens which are notable for the splendid harmony between natural scenery and plastic form.

GIOTTO (1267-1337)

Passing from his native Mugello to the Florentine school of Cimabue, and from here to an important period in Rome, Giotto brought to painting a current of profound renewal. The painted buildings of the backgrounds and the plastic emphasis of the figures in the Stories of St Francis in the Upper Basilica of Assisi betray in fact clear Cosmatesque influences and a certain hint of the art of Arnolfo di Cambio. Characteristics that would reappear, filtered by a more austere artistic maturity, in the frescoes of the Arena Chapel in Padua. Many of his works are to be found in Florence, where in 1334 Giotto was appointed chief architect of the Opera del Duomo.

LEONARDO DA VINCI (1452-1519)

Painter, Sculptor, Engineer, Writer and Scientist. Son of a notary, Leonardo left his native village of Vinci at the age of sixteen and moved to Florence where he attended the workshop of Verrocchio. Very soon his natural talent and thirst for knowledge took him beyond the confines of painting, in which he nevertheless proved himself to be the true champion of the revolution initiated by Masaccio. He moved from the Milan of the Sforza family to Mantua, and from Venice to Rome, with brief stays in Florence, and finally to the France of Louis XII and Francis I, where he died. He devoted himself to art, but also to mathematics, physics, biology, anatomy, and civil and hydraulic engineering, excelling as a sculptor, architect, scientist and writer; in short, he was the most ingenious and versatile personality of the Italian Renaissance.

LIPPI Filippino (1457-1504)
Painter. Filippino, the son of Filippo Lippi, was born in Prato but trained in Florence under Botticelli, who strongly influenced his early paintings. Called to complete the Brancacci Chapel in the church of the Carmine and to decorate the Carafa Chapel in Santa Maria sopra Minerva in Rome, his art revealed a resolute search for architectural grandiosity tempered however by classical moderation and a constant veil of profound melancholy, to which were added, in his later works, clear references to the painting of Leonardo.

LIPPI Filippo (1406-1469)
Painter. Filippo Lippi was born in Florence and when very young was able to follow the work of Masaccio and Masolino in the Brancacci Chapel of the Carmine, which left a strong impression on him. After working in Padua he returned to Florence where he devoted himself to an unending search for light effects, limpid colours and spatial depth, which initially brought him close to Beato Angelico though subsequently made him a precursor of Botticelli. As well as many paintings of a religious nature conserved in Florence and in Paris, noteworthy are the fresco cycles for the cathedrals of Prato and Spoleto, on whose execution he was working when he died.

MASACCIO (1401-1428)
Painter. Little is known about the background and life of Tommaso di Ser Giovanni di Simone Guidi, born in San Giovanni Valdarno, and mystery also surrounds his sudden death in Rome. Certainly he was, with Brunelleschi and Donatello, one of the protagonists of that artistic revolution that distinguished Florence in the early 15th century as a prelude to Humanism. He worked for a long time with Masolino da Panicale, who was also from Valdarno, and with him executed the frescoes of the Brancacci Chapel in the church of the Carmine, a fundamental reference-point for all later Renaissance painting.

MICHELANGELO (1475-1564)
Painter, Sculptor, Architect and Poet. Michelangelo was a highly versatile artist - sculptor, painter, architect and poet - who trained at the workshops of Florence, was esteemed by Lorenzo il Magnifico and was close to the leading Humanists of his time. He travelled a great deal, everywhere leaving extraordinary examples of his sublime art which was for long considered to be the perfect model of classical art itself: from the Vatican *Pietà* and the *Last Judgement* of the Sistine Chapel to the Captives and innumerable paintings. Perhaps his greatest achievement was that he succeeded in synthesizing a whole tradition stretching from the past up to Masaccio, re-elaborating the fundamental elements of it in a context of an emphatic and triumphant monumentality.

PAOLO UCCELLO (1397-1475)
Paolo di Dono, better known as Paolo Uccello, was a much talked-about painter in his native Florence due to his introverted character and his critical attitude towards the contemporary Florentine school. Educated in the Gothic tradition and influenced by an important journey to Venice, he favoured the use of vivid colours and exaggerated perspective effects which were vaguely medieval and in certain instances even unreal, as can be seen in his Florentine works, in Santa Maria Novella and in the Duomo, in the frescoes for Prato Cathedral, and in the masterpiece of his maturity, the Battle of San Romano.

VASARI Giorgio (1511-1574)
Architect and Writer. Born and raised in Arezzo, Vasari moved to Florence in 1504 to study in the workshop of Andrea del Sarto and Baccio Bandinelli. A visit to Rome in the retinue of Cardinal Ippolito de' Medici enabled him to learn from classical art and architecture, and a journey to Venice brought him into contact with Titian and other Venetian masters, but this did not influence the typical Tusco-Roman Mannerism that became the main hallmark of his art. Returning to Rome, where he remained until 1553, protected by Cardinal Alessandro Farnese, he met Michelangelo, who influenced him in his choice of devoting himself exclusively to architecture. Summoned again to Florence by Cosimo I de' Medici, for him he supervised the decoration of Palazzo Vecchio and built the Uffizi and the Vasari Corridor. But among his most famous works an important mention must be made of his monumental writing, the Lives of the Artists, an exhaustive collection of biographies of the leading Italian artists of his time.

VERROCCHIO (1430-1488)
Painter and Sculptor. The nickname by which Andrea di Cione is more commonly known recalls the goldsmith Giuliano Verrocchio, to whom he was apprenticed as a young man, but his fame has always been linked to his activity as a painter and above all as a sculptor who drew on the examples of great masters like Ghiberti, Filippo Lippi and Donatello. A protégé of the Medici family, who commissioned a large part of his production, in Florence he executed splendid works for Orsanmichele, the Baptistery and San Salvi, and in Venice the equestrian monument to Bartolomeo Colleoni in Campo Santi Giovanni e Paolo, which he worked on until his death in that city.

INDEX